THE MAMA-BEAR CEO

Heartfelt, straight talking strategies to help you manage your life and business.

By Coralie

Copyright © 2024 by Coralie

All rights reserved including the right of reproduction in whole or in part in any form.

This publication is designed to provide accurate and authoritative information in regard to the subject matter covered. It is sold with the understanding that neither the author nor the publisher is engaged in rendering legal, investment, accounting or other professional services. While the author has used their best efforts in preparing this book, they make no representations or warranties with respect to the accuracy or completeness of the contents of this book and specifically disclaim any implied warranties of merchantability or fitness for a particular purpose. No warranty may be created or extended by sales representatives or written sales materials. The advice and strategies contained herein may not be suitable for your situation. You should consult with a professional when appropriate. Neither the publisher nor the author shall be liable for any loss of profit or any other commercial damages, including but not limited to special, incidental, consequential, personal, or other damages.

Coralie

@The Mama Bear CEO

Cover photo credit: Amanda Clarke, Amanda Clarke Photography

Be careful what you become in the pursuit of what you want...

CONTENTS

Prologue 5
About the author and a note on AI 8
Chapter 1. Who are you? 10
Chapter 2. The Mama-Bear CEO 21
Chapter 3. Your biggest problem 30
Chapter 4. Lets get real 44
Chapter 5. Environment dictates Performance 60
Chapter 6. Know your Numbers 70
Chapter 7. Is it all too much? 84
Chapter 8. Are you bubbling in perturbation? 101
Chapter 9. It's all about the systems 108
Chapter 10. Some of my favourite systems 119
Chapter 11. It's about the non-negotiables 125
Chapter 12. So you want to be rich? 131
Chapter 13. 86400 138
Chapter 14. Numbers & Feelings 154
Some lessons in images 161
Acknowledgements 166
Resources 169

Prologue

This whole book fell out of my head this morning, whilst I was cycling on Florence, my sky-blue beach cruiser complete with wicker basket adorned with a vine of silk roses around the edge. I was coming back from my daughter's hair and beauty salon, having opened up for her as she was feeling ill. The sun was shining and I was, unusually, taking a day for myself. My partner Sean was away and the kids were off doing other things and so typically my plans had to change so I could help Lauren. But rather than feeling hacked off, I enjoyed the chance to ride my bike and because of that I birthed this project.

Which just shows that you don't need all your little duckies lined up in a row to get new ideas out there. The best ones often happen when you're least expecting them. (Probably because you're not putting yourself under any pressure and they can pop up like happy bubbles!).

I know that in our world right now there is a lot of fear and worry about 'stability' and finances and for many families things are a real struggle with the increased cost of living and job losses through redundancy or company closures. Many more people are turning inwards and taking their lives in their hands, rather than relying on someone else for their future security and so new businesses are being born every minute of every day. Whether you're setting up another stream of income on top of your current job, or you're going 'all-in' on a new venture, know that this is for you. I was exactly where you are right now and from side hustles to full blown companies, I have started from the very beginning of them all, full of fear, lacking in knowledge and no money to spare. But I promise you, if you stay focussed, do the right things and open your eyes and hearts to learning, you can succeed.

So to all you beautiful people out there who might be wondering how on earth you can manage to run your businesses, or you're feeling inadequate or like you're failing, read on. I've got a few tips up my sleeve to help you navigate through all of this with less stress, more energy and some smart ways to stay on top of it all. Watch out for the little icons for my favourite ones and be sure to highlight yours too. Use this book as a workbook to guide you and if you get a bit distracted, enjoy the colouring sections top and bottom of each page to brighten up your day!

About the author and a note on AI

At the time of writing, Coralie has skidded into her 50's and realised that the last 20 years have flashed by so fast that steps need to be taken to stop panic from setting in because there's so much life left to live! She is blessed with her partner Sean, children Lauren, Toby, Max, Lucy and Ava (all blended together but that's a story for another book) and appears to have accidentally set up a retirement home for elderly Bichon Frise dogs with two of them currently in residence. She has run several successful companies of her own in the SaaS and Publishing industries, having previously enjoyed a career as a Global Project Manager for various bluechips including IBM, run companies for other people and throughout all her careers has enjoyed content writing and customer care. She now enjoys coaching and implementing business solutions for small business owners (who are her favourites because they're generally the most passionate).

She loves animals, riding her bicycle or motorbike to coffee shops, writing, journaling and being warm. Tea is an everyday staple as well as a good selection of notepads and stationery, because what else is there in life? Oh, probably a glass of cold champagne, gardening and the sun. Because all of those things are simple and, when it boils down to it, are actually all you need.

   Ps - this is future-Coralie here. I'm just proofing this book before it goes off to print and wanted to add a small piece on my thoughts on AI. Quite simply I really wish it didn't exist. I cannot believe we have entered a world where we are allowing technology to take over an area of our enjoyment where our words do not come from our own hearts or minds but instead are scraped off the internet by software and regurgitated like second hand porridge. I want you to know that AI hasn't been anywhere near these words, nor will I let it come close to any writing I do simply because I don't believe it is honest nor 'real'. I want you to know that I'm sat at my desk, in my cabin at the bottom of the garden, typing these pages on a mechanical keyboard plugged into my Mac, watching a robin hop around on the tree outside, occasionally looking at me through the window.
   Connection to you, the reader, should be genuine. So please know that despite my acute wrist tendonitis, and beginning of what is most likely arthritis, I will continue to wear out a keyboard a year, rather than succumb to the ease of AI.

   Let's go.

Chapter 1. Who are you?

This book is for you if you have a yearning to do something for yourself. If there's a niggle every time you go to work that you could be creating your own path, not having to sit through endless meetings or wasting hours of your life on a commute that you hate. If you're chucking your kids through the door of daycare before you screech into your job by the skin of your teeth, jumping onto zoom calls with the camera off because you're stuck in traffic or simply gazing out of the window because you know there's a better way.

This is for you if you have already made the jump and are wondering how on earth everyone else seems to manage. The never ending juggle with money, social media posts, long hours and staff who are so entitled that you wonder why you ever started this.

Or if you're running a halfway house of part time CEO and miserably employed, this is certainly for you. Because I'm going to show you why this is the worst position to be in and what you need to do to get out of it.

Most of all, this book is for anyone wondering why life and business all feels so hard, even though you're the CEO of both.

Let's do a little discovery session.

First of all, it's important to note that this book has been purposely designed for you to write in! It has been developed as a workbook for you to make notes, colour in, doodle and enjoy and to give you a resource that you can come back to time and again.

There are 'Mama Bear Tips' (with the best ones clearly highlighted) and space for you to dream and plan. Grab yourself some pens and colours so that you can get properly stuck in. If you've bought the kindle edition then hop on over to my instagram page, (@themamabearceo), give it a follow and download the workbook so you've got somewhere to store your notes.

So, if you've ever worked for a blue-chip or a company with a good onboarding and HR department, it's likely you will have completed some sort of personality tests where you analyse your strengths and weaknesses. There are so many to choose including Clifton Strengths, Myers-Briggs and more recently Human Design which is complex but very insightful. One thing I've realised is that it's no good just doing these things once in your career. Do them regularly - they don't always stay the same and they can be pretty useful in determining why you are behaving in certain ways and why some things feel harder than others.

What I'd like you to do now is pick one of these and go and complete it. Clifton Strengths, the full paid version, is really fab as it gives you a list of your 34 strengths, in descending order and it can be a real eye opener (and it's really accurate too). Go on, make a cup of tea, log on and find the survey… get your results then read on.

So how did you do? Find out anything interesting about yourself? I bet you found the results uncannily accurate! Don't put them away in a drawer though. You can make up some graphics or even a poster for your wall to help you focus on what you are brilliant at, and not to worry too much about what you're not. Take 10 minutes to pop something together in Canva and celebrate your uniqueness! Otherwise jot down the key takeaways here:

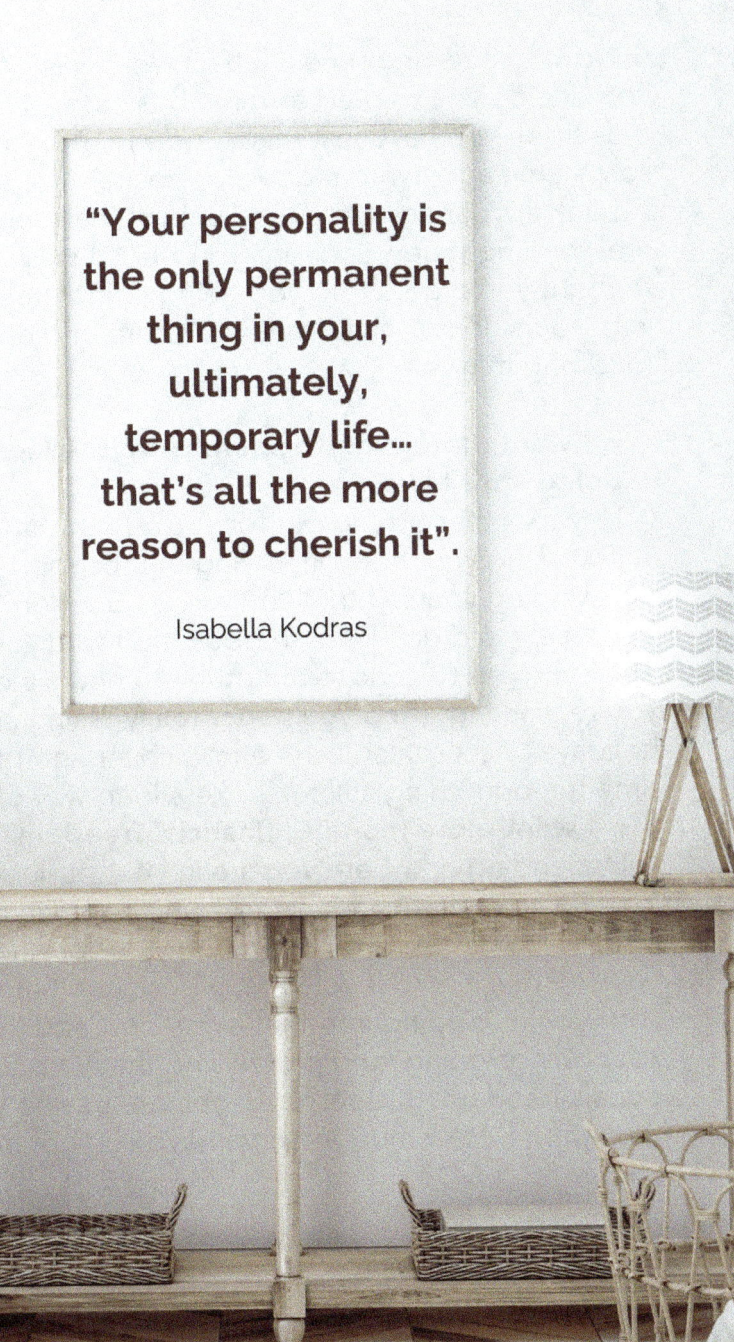

"Your personality is the only permanent thing in your, ultimately, temporary life... that's all the more reason to cherish it".

Isabella Kodras

Now, let's rewind time a little. What was it that made you decide you wanted to run a business? Whether it's a decision you have just made, or one that you made some time ago, write it down opposite.

Look at your answer. Do you think that the way you are living right now is giving you what it was that you thought you'd get? Are you being completely honest with yourself? It's likely that you wrote one of the following things:

- **I want more time to spend with the kids/family/doing stuff I like.**

How has that played out for you? I bet that you are still working your nuts off, diving out for sports days and kidding yourself that you've got 'freedom' because you didn't have to book it off with your boss. Then you get to choose the other 18 hours a day you're working. And you're not really taking any holidays because you can't afford cover and the whole time freedom thing still feels like a long way off.

- **I want more money / financial freedom.**

Depending on where you are in your business journey I wonder if you have achieved this yet. I would also like to bet that you're probably not paying yourself much, and if you're in a business that takes cash you're dipping into that every now and then to keep things going, and pretending that your turnover equals freedom. It doesn't. If you are paying yourself then great! How much reserve have you got in the bank?

- **I can do a better job than my old boss.**

This one is probably true. But answer me this. If you thought about how you're looking after yourself and your business, would you employ you?

- **Because I want to be successful.**

Have you actually ever, truly, defined what this means to you? And have you considered what you'll be prepared to do in order to make this happen? Or is this more of a vanity trip for your ego to see your name on something? (If at this point you think I'm being harsh, just know I'm known for my straight talking. Someone has to say it, and often it's looking at the uncomfortable truths that allow you to make changes for the better. Know this is said with love and don't go switching off because you'd rather listen to your mates who won't hold the mirror up for you....)

What I have realised during my years in business, is that we often go into something with great ideas, but they quite quickly disappear under a pile of 'stuff' that hadn't been considered because the dream was bigger than the planning. And life can get in the way and before you know it you're months or years into what can feel like a noose around your neck. Those giddy nights of imagining your own business turn into sleepless ones wondering how you're going to pay for maternity cover (either for yourself or your staff), or how you can pay the rent when the rates have just gone up again, or how you're sick of social media and people talking shit about you on reviews for no reason at all....

What's your reality right now in comparison to this dream? Be honest. Write it down here:

Now write down what your ultimate business goal is. What's the thing that makes you tingle and can't wait to get started?

OK. More tea. Let's take a look at all the core areas of your world and we'll tackle them one by one.

It isn't going to be easy.
But will it be worth it?
Hell yes!

Stay with me for the journey.   I'll be right here holding your hand and cheering you on.

Chapter 1 Review and Actions - Who are you?

- If you're reading on a Kindle version then download the workbook from @themamabearceo on Instagram so you can do the written activities.
- Do an online personality test such as Clifton Strengths.
- Create a little graphic or simply print out your top strengths and give these some thought.
- Think about what it was that made you start, or want to start, your own business.
- Think about your current reality - is it matching that dream?
- What is your big, ultimate goal for your life and business?

Chapter 2. The Mama-Bear CEO

Now we know a little bit more about who you are, let me tell you a short story about me and why I decided to write this book.

At school I was compliant. My writing was neat, my books were beautifully presented and I never once got a detention. I feared getting things wrong and I was in the 'normal' group of kids. I was never cool. I had spots and hair that struggled before the advent of GHD's. My achievements were gained through sheer hard work and I thought that I needed to tick the right boxes to succeed.

It has taken me until the last 7 years or so for me to realise what an utter crock of crap that was. The school system is failing our kids, we are not learning anything of any use at all and we are being taught, essentially, to take orders.

I probably knew this in me, deep down, which is why I spent so long miserably employed and then started my own 'proper' business at the age of 32. Yes, it took me that long to get my act together to go for it. Prior to that I had so many ideas of what I could do, but the 'security' offered to me by my Project Managers job at IBM held me hostage. Resentment for the glass ceiling built up (yes, I hit it damned hard and got stuck there. I often wondered if, looking down, I metaphorically appeared like a fish under ice, slowly opening my mouth wide to try and gulp some air, but never being able to find the hole to break through).

I started a publishing company in my spare time. Looking back now I wonder what on earth I was thinking. I did a full time job in compressed hours Tuesday-Thursday and with a 14 year old and 1 year old to look after I somehow thought I had capacity to create a monthly magazine. I guess the point of this is that you have to start somewhere. There is never the perfect time (although looking back there are some better than others) and if you believe in yourself enough then you can make it happen.

The magazine grew to two monthly titles and I was still working full time having had my second daughter (and third child) by this point. She was still a baby and I was getting more and more exhausted. Taking Valium to get me on business flights as I was so terrified of flying, leaving for the airport at 4.30 in the morning, working through until really late to get everything done…. it took my sister to look me straight in the face after I'd missed a funeral to catch up on work and ask if I was OK for me to realise something had to stop.

This was the moment I had to choose. I was straddling a full time 'secure' job whilst running my own business and on another batch of anti-depressants to get me through. I figured if I launched another title, I could bring in enough to cover the essentials plus a bit extra and then I would have made the leap away from employment.

Since then, I have never looked back. And I quickly realised the utter sham that is the myth of employment security. I had effectively abdicated my future to someone else for so, so long and it was time to change. I'd done enough learning on someone else's time and money and now I had to put one foot in front of the other and get on with it for myself.

Are you currently in a limbo situation where you are clinging on to 'safety' with a paycheque, as well as trying to squeeze in your future dreams with a side hustle in your spare time?

It's funny how when you let something go, another thing will come in to fill the void. It wasn't long after I had been running my publishing company full time that I had one of my infamous 'shower moments'. For clarity, they're not some sort of porn/Only Fans situation, I'm talking 10 minutes of solitude under running water where my brain offloads all its thoughts and oftentimes I'll get all my good ideas first thing in the morning!

It hit me like a face-slap that I was running my business like an utter spanner. Somehow I was cobbling things together, using spreadsheets, a huge supply of post it notes and too many email addresses to run something quite simple.

The first lesson I learned here was this.

What I mean by that is how many of us just 'make do' or fudge things to get by, and then carry on like that? Our businesses deserve better! We deserve better!

So that morning, in the shower, my brain quickly connected the dots from everything I had learned and implemented in my time as an IT Project Manager and I came up with a blueprint for what my business needed.

It took me about 30 minutes to swallow the embarrassment that it had taken me this long to realise that I was running my business like a coffee table hobby and just because I was working from a home office, it didn't mean my business was any less viable. I spruced up my attitude, dusted off my desk and set to work.

Now I appreciate that not everyone is going to create a spin-off business in order to get their existing one into order. That's what this book is for - to save you from going through all that hard work! But what I did was create some software, to run my business, that I then went on to sell to every other publisher, just like me across the world, so that they could better run their businesses too. I filled a gap in the market for an online software solution that allowed publishers to see, in real time, what their businesses were doing. And since then, helping people has been my passion. Sticking a bag over your head and ear plugs in and hoping for the best does not make for a successful business. And trust me, even if you can't hear the noise, things will quickly catch up with you if you ignore them.

So what happened in the last 7 years that has made me change how I feel about things… and why the Mama-Bear CEO?

In a nutshell I collapsed.

My body stopped me from gruelling working hours.

It stopped me from never saying 'no'.

It stopped me from taking on way too much work.

And it made me realise, very quickly, how you take your health for granted the whole time until it is taken away.

It took me a year, and constant effort every day even now, to get back my energy and my health. From spending nearly six months unable to do anything and just sleeping on the sofa I'm now back to what looks like, on the face of it, a normal menopausal woman!

But just underneath the skin, and firmly at the front of my thoughts, are the scars of what working too hard and thinking I was invincible can do to you.

Life shouldn't be like that.

It is too short.

We can be smarter.

I will now defend whatever work I do, company that I run or people that I love as a Mama-Bear. I have a built in instinct to nurture and protect and to wrap an arm around those I care about, all the while retaining a fun and ambitious edge.

My skill set is diverse. My personality even more so. Which makes my role as CEO so perfect and I know it's perfect for you too.

Because no matter what day it is, or what you're having to do, as women we are able to pop on whatever hat is needed. We can turn our hands to so many different things. And before you think there are others out there doing it better than you, trust me, whether they are or not, it doesn't matter.

What matters is your own heart.

Your own health.

Your own path.

Are you risking your own health (mental or physical), your family and relationships or your future dreams and desires by sitting in limbo-camp waiting for something to happen?

Are you too scared to make the leap into being self-employed?

Think about where you're at, right now, in terms of where your efforts are going and if this is setting you on the path to freedom and dreams or is this taking you further into the clutches of 'safe' and away from the ability to make your own money and rules?

Start being true to yourself and lets get on with this journey!

Chapter 2 Review and Actions - The Mama Bear CEO

- Are you in a state of limbo between a paid job of perceived safety and your dreams?
- Think about what you're risking by being in this halfway house and how much pressure it is putting on you and your relationships. Think about where you are right now and how you want this to change.

Chapter 3. Your biggest problem

My business coach, Ian Dickson, is a wonderful gentleman who has a toolkit filled with everything he needs to address most situations. I have learned many lessons from his calm and knowledgeable demeanour, one of which is to not switch on your 'I know' button.

We are all guilty of this. We read something, hear something or see something and instantly think that we've seen it before and so we don't need to absorb it again. Occasionally this will be true. But sometimes, if you switch that button on too quickly, you'll miss out on a pearl that might just help you.

This is one of those chapters. You might think you already know what your biggest problem is. You might be working out all sorts of challenges to get where you want to be and you might think you've got risk assessments coming out of your ears so you're sorted. But I am pretty sure that most of our problems generally come down to one thing.

Fear.

Whilst it might not always be obvious, it's fear that is most often the root cause of most of our issues. (And I guarantee this is where the Extroverts in the group will dispute this and say that fear rarely comes and I'll say it does, you're just better at kidding yourself!).

Think about where you are right now. The journey you have taken to get there. Things you've navigated on the way.

Be honest - how many decisions have you either made, or not made, because of fear or worry? Thoughts like:

- What will people think?
- What if it goes wrong?
- I'm not qualified enough
- I don't have the money
- It isn't possible
- I'm too young/old
- Nobody does this
- There's too much competition
- I don't know what I'm doing
- I'm not good enough

Lets do a little exercise. Nobody is watching. Write down here some of the things that scare you:

How would you feel if you didn't have these fears?
What would it do to your life and your business?

Shall I let you into a secret?
You can make them all go away, right now.
And you know that, right?

Fears aren't real. They may feel like it but it's totally your imagination that has created them. It's the voices in your head that keep telling you there's a problem, when in reality there really isn't one at all. You might think it is all very real, because your brain has a very clever way of creating a fight or flight response which triggers a physical sensation due to the stress hormones released and so it's an uncomfortable feeling that you want to avoid.But, Mama Bear, you are stronger than that!

Instead of focussing on the fear and negativity, start practising some positivity. There are lots of books you can read that will teach you how to do this but in a nutshell, try implementing some of the following:

* Before you go to bed, write down three things that you are grateful for. This will reaffirm to your brain a positive message and help you feel less fearful. Have a go by doing that now.
* Remember that your subconscious cannot distinguish between positive or negative language. So if it is constantly hearing 'I don't want to be poor' it will just hear the word 'poor' and because it doesn't do negatives it will just hear 'I want to be

poor'. It also believes everything you tell it so all those things you tell yourself become stored up as fact! Change the way you speak about yourself and situations so that it is always positive. It's a tough one to do and it takes practice but it really makes a difference.

* Don't allow other peoples worries to fill your head. Whenever they seep in, imagine the arms of a penny-slot machine scooping it all away.
* Go to bed earlier and get better sleep. There is a direct correlation between decreased depression and anxiety (and therefore overall mental health) when you have a good nights sleep vs burning the candle at both ends. Wonder why fear is always worse at night? It's because your brain needs time to sleep and process thoughts - essentially it needs to shut down and recalibrate - and if you keep it up worrying about 'what if's' it has way too much to deal with!

I mentioned earlier about needing Valium to fly. This is one of my fears and trust me, it's a very deep rooted, very, very real issue. I used to have to travel a bit for work and that meant, on occasion, flying. I have a huge fear of heights, crashing, death… and being in a bean tin 30,000 feet up is really not my idea of fun.

This went on for many years. I would never NOT fly but to turn up to a meeting looking like the snake off the Jungle Book is not ideal, especially coupled with a 'few large ones' just to take the edge off. I nearly missed my best friends wedding in Vegas because of the thought of the flight, until I gave myself a strict talking to and went anyway.

So I decided to tackle the fear head on. I tried (in no particular order):

- Tapping
- Alcohol
- Drugs
- Hypnotherapy
- Meditation
- Anchor Bands
- Learning about what happens on a plane

And they all helped, to a point. But they didn't stop the gut surging, sweat inducing panic that would come over me when I walked down the tube to board or whenever the plane did anything other than stay still. I've been moved on a plane before because I was worrying other passengers with my sobbing and my most embarrassing moment was when a crew member recognised me from a previous flight and commented that I was 'doing a lot better today'!

Then one day I got on a plane utterly cold turkey. It was by accident, of course, but by design from my partner who was blissfully unaware at this point in our relationship just how bad I could be on a plane. He had lovingly booked my 40th birthday surprise - a break in Egypt so I could fulfil my dream of swimming up to a bar to order a drink. He packed all my luggage in secret (the only thing he forgot was my flip flops!) and despite warnings from the girls in the office about my 'flight meds' he figured we'd be just fine.

Of course, all the while I'm on the ground and nowhere near the plane, it's all happy days! And oh my gosh, the thought of landing somewhere hot and sunny always fills my heart with joy. But unfortunately for Sean, by the time we had boarded (and fyi this was before you could pre-book seats on EasyJet) we ended up separated with an aisle and two rows apart. Watching me sobbing on take off like a four year old was heartbreaking as he couldn't reach me. Nobody would swap seats. I'd had no booze, no Valium and the fear surging through my legs and my stomach was like nothing ever before. We didn't make the same mistake on the way home and made sure we were sat together. But this time he held my hand. And I breathed and held onto him and the fear reduced, just a little.

Then the next time was a little better and so on... What did I do to help remove the fear?

- Every time we fly I have a little routine and one of the things I do is reward myself with a small bottle of bubbly and a gift from the airplane catalogue if I've managed to stay calm!
- I visualise that my flight will be good. I make a CHOICE that my time in the air is going to be time for ME - I want to feel relaxed and at ease instead of wasting so many hours in a state of panic.
- I remind myself that fear does not change ANYTHING. Does my being scared affect the turbulence? No.
- Does my being scared affect the speed of takeoff? No.
- Does my knowledge about the first 40 seconds of the flight affect the outcome? No. (For those with the same fear, you'll know about those 40 seconds.

So wait for the bump and then you'll know it's plain sailing after that!).

Knowing I can't change any of this, I might as well sit back, get on with it and enjoy it. I'm making it sound a little straightforward but in all honesty that's what you have to do. Just stop it!

I managed to do a long haul flight to Perth by myself a few years back. I admit I had a bit of a freak out when I landed at Singapore on the way home but then on the final leg I fell asleep. That has NEVER happened on any flight, long or short haul and shows just how far I've come in controlling my mind with it all.

- What is it that is frightening you?
- What is the likelihood of it happening?
- What is the worst that could actually happen?

I generally end up narrowing everything down to 'well will I, or someone else die' and if the answer is 'no' then get on with it!

And I suppose the simplest answer is 'do I like feeling like this?'. And if you don't then just decide to do something about it.

The biggest bat you can use to swat a fear is to ACT. DOING something is the most powerful antidote to smacking that fear right in the face. Doing nothing allows it to fester, to get bigger so that ultimately it enshrouds us and paralyses us. Also remember that the opposite emotion to fear is excitement so every time you feel something scary try and think of it as being excited - the feeling is actually very similar and by using this in a positive way it can lift you up to tackle that 'scary thing' head on!

There is one particular fear that I want to cover. I've used my fear of flying as a way of explaining how to get over something debilitating, that doesn't always make sense yet feels very real. But the one I want to focus on now is probably one of the biggest, and most dangerous ones in our lives.

And that's the fear of what others might think.

Stop for a moment and give yourself some time to consider this. Can you honestly, hand on heart, say that you are, and have, lived your life totally to your tune? Have you stayed true to yourself and your dreams and desires or have you allowed peer pressure, worry or thoughts about what someone else might think influence your decisions? Are the clothes you wear the ones you love, or the ones you think you should be wearing? Is the car you drive the one that makes you smile in the mornings or does it tick a social box, that's costing you 100's each month just for the 'likes'?

Ever more pressure is on us now to perform for the Gram, to have perfect houses, routines or wardrobes. And yet none of those things will make us happy if they're not in alignment with our souls. Trust me, you might feel good about 'fitting in' for a while. And that 'while' could literally be years and years. But one day something will happen and you'll stop and realise how you've missed out on experiences and feelings because of decisions that you've made because of someone else. Who is no doubt running their own lives, doing what they choose and they genuinely don't give a damn about yours. They'll have long forgotten about that Facebook post you nervously put up suggesting that you might be doing XYZ. It's chip paper! Think about it this way. Do you actually spend too much time nit picking about what everyone else is doing? (If you do then please take a look at yourself!). It's likely that you have a vague interest for all of 5 minutes but then you turn away and get on with what's important to you. This is what everyone else does! So stop with the comparisons.

Stop with the fear of judgement and stop with feeling inadequate. You are you. This is your journey and nobody else's.

After all, without being too morose about it, what if you were told that you could do whatever you liked without judgement because your time on this earth was limited? What if nobody actually cared and you were free to pursue your dreams because nobody was watching? Would you be living life a little differently then? You'll kick yourself big time if you suddenly found out that life was shorter than you thought it might be - you can't claw that time back and I bet that 'Jacqui from Bristol' doesn't actually give a toss whether you chose the vintage Beetle or the white CLK - the only thing she'd probably say is 'aww babe <care emoji>, hugs' before she flicks onto an ad from Anthropologie.

Bob from Sussex isn't likely to come and help you at 3am when you've woken up again because you're depressed - everything you feel inside of you has to be dealt with by you, no matter who you've shared it with.

Stop making choices through fear of what others might say. Because you'll end up paying the ultimate price long after those people will ever realise you weren't happy in the first place.

Chapter 3 Review and Actions - Your biggest problem

- Write down the things that are scaring you.
- How would you feel if you didn't have these fears?
- Get a journal to keep by the side of your bed to record your gratitudes before you go to sleep each night.
- Give though to your thoughts. Your subconscious believes everything so think about what you're telling it!
- Go to bed earlier and prioritise your sleep. That's when all the healing happens!
- Think about what scares you and what you can do about these fears.

Chapter 4. Lets get real

So now that we've established that you're in the driving seat (and let's be clear, this is not so that you can bulldoze over everyone in your path. We do this with grace and care), shall we get on with sorting out the next problem?

It's to do with how you treat yourself and your business. Whether you have self-worth issues, lack of time, a chaotic head or any other reason you care to mention, I've seen so many business owners look after their most precious assets really badly. It's not intentional of course, most people don't actually realise they're doing it. Whether it's the freedom of not having anyone looking over your shoulder, or because you're a grown up and there are other things taking priority, so many of us seem to be utterly winging it when it comes to these things. And particularly as women, we often put ourselves to the bottom of the pile, allowing everyone else's needs and wants to be dealt with before ours. Got kids? How many of your partners treat having their own children for the day like a childminding job? Are you taking all the burden for managing everything in the house and your family? Is your business seen as a cute hobby so it isn't taken seriously?

There are so many factors that can come into play but the bottom line is this. If you want to succeed and have a long and happy life, you MUST prioritise yourself first. Then, depending on the circumstances it's either business or family next and it's your judgement call as to how that works on any given day. But for goodness sake stop doing everything half-arsed, or at least good enough. What can you do to make things better?

Well first of all, lets remind ourselves of our ultimate goal. You might want to go back to the beginning of the book to remind yourself of what this is or take more time now to think about what the goal should be, now you've learned a thing or two about fear! Write your ultimate goal down here:

Whilst we're on the subject of goals, let me tell you a secret. Most people are absolutely rubbish about setting goals. They either:
Pick something way too simple
Pick something that is utterly impossible
Choose something that makes them feel good
Focus on a figure that looks great on motivational wallpaper but does nothing else other than puff ego

Or

Set a goal and then forget about it because it wasn't really what they wanted in the first place.
Learning how to set goals is critical for new businesses. Please don't go off and waste energy writing a business plan either. By the time you've executed on one of your ideas you'll most likely end up at a destination that you hadn't even dreamed of (if you're good at listening to your customer feedback) and the plan will have gone awol by the second paragraph. If your business idea is based on solid enough research, then get on with it and set your goals to guide you.
You'll have heard about 'SMART' goals which are:
- Specific
- Measurable
- Attainable
- Relevant

- Time bound

Which is a useful method to get your head around what a goal looks like. But in my mind, the most important thing is whether or not the goal is linked to your bigger WHY (in other words your main goal). If you've never watched 'will it make the boat go faster' then search on YouTube for the video by Ben Hunt-Davis who was part of an underachieving Men's Eight boat team. He explains how they set themselves a crazy goal of winning an Olympic Medal within just two years and how their whole way of working was challenged with the simple question of 'Will it make the boat go faster?'. And if it did, then the actions towards that goal would be executed and if not they'd try something different. Remember that when you're executing a goal, which you need to have broken down into a set of manageable steps, that it is the journey itself which is important, not just hitting the target. There's nothing worse than flogging yourself for 90 days, falling out with your family and ending up with stress headaches to hit your goal and metaphorically pull a sad old party popper at the end with no enjoyment attached.

Some tips for setting goals:
- No matter what the goal, you have to EXECUTE to make it happen. Goals take work!
- Goals need breaking down into manageable chunks to avoid overwhelm. Want to lose 2 stone? Break it up into pounds per week and work out your deadline.
- Don't be vague. If you had a magic wand and one wish to tell a 5 year old Genie, you'd sure as heck be really clear with your message!

- Financial goals feel important and exciting. And they have their place. But actually it's the emotional ones, and the ones where you give SERVICE that tend to work better. Because you don't want to let people down and your business, I'm sure, is designed to serve a need. Do that exceptionally well and your goals will inadvertently translate into financial success anyway.
- Set goals which are important to you and align with your beliefs, but don't make them so easy that it doesn't give you a bit of a tingle when you think about them!
- Enjoy using good old pen and paper to brainstorm, map out and plan your goals.
- Find someone who can help keep you accountable and on track when you set your goal.

Ok, so with the above in mind, write your ultimate goal down again here:

Now lets jot down all the barriers that are stopping you from doing this:

OK. There will always be challenges. There is very rarely a smooth path to success but listen up.

"By taking care of ourselves first and foremost it ensures that our care for others ultimately can come from a place of inner abundance, a feeling of already being taken care of from within. As a result, we become more giving partners, family members, friends and beyond'.

Looking after yourself is not selfish. There is a huge difference here and one that many of us don't consider. This isn't about being self absorbed or not thinking of others. This is about treating yourself as you want others to treat you and if you do this you will see people's behaviour towards you change.

Putting yourself first builds confidence. This helps to improve your life. And people like being around confident (not arrogant) people so you will attract good people to you.

Having enough energy to feel good about yourself and what you're doing allows you to help others.

You'll quickly realise that not everyone is forever. Let people go who are toxic, fake, judgemental… and thank them for the lessons they have taught you. The space they leave will be quickly filled by the right people.

Have a think about this for a minute and answer these questions using the sliding scale:

* Do you make sure that you eat proper, nourishing foods 80% of the time?

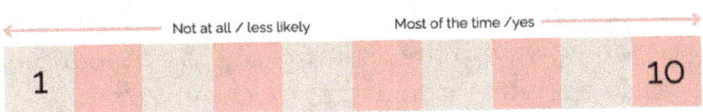

* Do you get to bed at the same time, consistently and have enough sleep?

* Do you have time to yourself each week to focus on a hobby or sport that you enjoy?

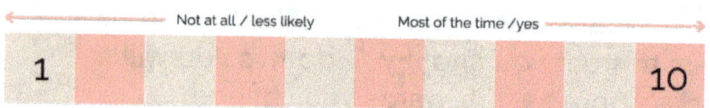

* Do you make time for exercise each day? (This can be a walk outside or a full blown cardio session at the gym).

* Are you drinking enough water?

* Honest one - how much alcohol are you drinking (and don't give me the bollocks of 'it's not that much because everyone drinks that much nowadays'). Write it down here, every glass for the week.

● Are you relying on cigarettes, recreational drugs or other things to keep you feeling sane?

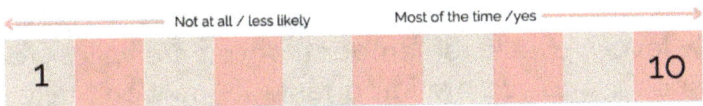

● Do you often feel on the verge of anger/anxiety/depression?

● Does work eat into every pore of your life, feeling like you hate it and you dream of a 'mild leg break' so that you can have an enforced stay in hospital?

● Do you have some physical symptoms that you've been ignoring because they're not too bad that, deep down, you know need addressing?

Take a look at your answers. If this was your son or daughter, how would these make you feel? What would you want to say to them? Is it any less valid because it's YOU?

My lovely, please remember that you are valid. You are special and you are important. If you won't take care of yourself then who will?

Go and make yourself some tea, or coffee and step outside for a moment. Make a promise to yourself that RIGHT NOW things are going to change. No matter what your circumstances, no matter how big the challenge. You can stop for 10 minutes and get some air and decide that today you are going to make a change.

From the list of things you've scored above, pick your top three.

Write them here.

And now, Mama Bear says you can pick just one. Because what you focus on gets results. Just one. We are not going to overwhelm or reduce your ability to succeed.

Go on. Just one. Write it here.

This is what you're going to focus on to get you started. Because, as L'Oreal said, 'you're worth it'.

Now let me share a story with you.

This is my tale, and will go some way to explaining why I'm so passionate about your health and wellbeing (and to all of my customers who are reading this you'll better understand why I bang on so much about this in our sessions together!).

In 2017 we took our first 'plane' holiday together as a family. Taking 4 kids away is no mean feat from a cost perspective but we were super excited to be visiting our eldest, Lauren, who was working another season as a hairdresser in Ibiza. This was a well timed break for us - Sean and I had undertaken a massive house renovation on top of running a couple of businesses and managing our busy home and so we were both pretty exhausted. Time in the sun was much needed and we enjoyed a fun week with the kids playing in the sea and floating on a giant unicorn. Which was the perfect antidote to stress and chaos!

Trigger warning - road accident references ahead.

We had only been home a few hours when my mobile rang. I thought Lauren was checking to see that we had got back OK but unusually I heard her friends voice on the line. 'There's been an accident' I was told. Our daughter had been involved in a hit and run and was still on the road, unconscious. I went into control mode.

'Is she breathing'.

'Have you contacted emergency services'.

'Has she vomited'.

And so it went. In a blur I pulled out our dirty clothes from one bag, shoving in clean ones whilst arranging new flights and care for our kids. We were on a plane the next day to get back to her in ITU.

I'll miss out the rest as it's not the point of my story, suffice to say that we are incredibly lucky that she survived, she has mostly healed and in our view got a little bit of a software upgrade after some brain bleeds!

What happened during our walks to and from the hospital though changed our lives. Lauren's accident was the 'straw that broke the camel's back' as the analogy goes (literally hers, and metaphorically ours). We realised that we had built a world that was crazy busy, and probably a little bit like the Three Little Piggies - with a huff and a puff our house could be blown down easier than we believed - and with this big puff we both realised we couldn't take much more.

I was already navigating my busy life with autoimmune issues and whilst a big lifestyle change had made a huge difference, we both knew that we weren't really doing enough for our health. Because we had slipped back into feeling mostly ok and so we went back to our default of going at a million miles an hour, constantly striving to achieve success. What had we done?

We had removed toxins from our home.

I changed all my cleaning and self care products to be natural.

I tried to cut out most sugar and we cooked from scratch.

But we hadn't slowed down.

We had stopped listening again.

We forgot how to say 'no' and we thought we were infallible.

We were a car-crash waiting to happen.

And then it actually did.

So we took another step back and worked out what we should do next.

- We decided to prioritise our health again.
- We became more strict about sleep.
- We took daily walks.
- We used essential oils for both our emotional and our physical needs (and to this day I haven't needed to see a GP for many, many years).

* We used the oils to help Laurens' recovery when she came back to the UK and we literally use them all the time, from treating infections to getting me on a plane and staying calm. If you want to find out more about how life-changing these are then simply drop me a line. I'd be pleased to have a chat about your world and see how I can help make it better.

Either way, don't ignore your body. It will give you signals to let you know that something is out of whack. Remember you have an intuition for a reason. Take some quiet time to 'listen in'. Try doing Yoga Nidra if you need some structure for this - it will help you scan your body. Don't brush off those niggles, because if you do it's likely that they will turn into a bigger niggle the longer you leave them.

Your beautiful mind and body is the only one you've got. And trust me, your health is YOUR responsibility. Without it you'll be really annoyed that you didn't listen. That spreadsheet, or proposal, or social media post can wait because as a business owner, whilst it's all on your shoulders, it's your shoulders that need to be strong.

Take care of you.

Chapter 4 Review and Actions - Let's get real

* Remind yourself of your ultimate life and business goal.
* Look at how to set goals and now re-write your life and business goal.
* Consider all the barriers you have to achieving this goal.
* Answer all the self care questions.
* Pick the top three areas where you need to focus more on looking after yourself.
* Then pick just one that you're going to give it your all.

Chapter 5. Environment dictates Performance

For many of us this is vital. Yet others don't feel it matters. What I've learned is that actually this really does play a part for everybody.

Lets take a look at how you're living and working right now.

Do you have a dedicated space where you can focus on your work? This applies whether you are an online expert with just a MacBook and headphones, or run a shop. Everybody needs some space to manage paperwork, thoughts, planning and the 'stuff' that comes with running a business. Does this space make you feel good? Does it help you with the tasks you have to do? Are the things you need neatly laid out or stored so that you're not ferreting around trying to find a pen?

I appreciate that I come from the group of people who think that stationery is one of our 5-a-day and that storage boxes are way up there with necessary life support items. So all of this stuff comes naturally to me. And I also appreciate that there are people who claim to like mess and 'piles of papers'. But I don't believe that clutter, dirt and mayhem are conducive to doing your best work. It's not the be-all and end-all but putting some effort into keeping things organised will pay dividends down the line.

If your home is chaos, chances are you'll be wasting a tonne of time trying to find things which generally raises your blood pressure out of sheer frustration. This has a knock-on effect to the rest of your day and can make you late if you have deadlines.

Dirt for most people reminds them that the cleaning needs to be done (another thing to store in your head on the 'to do' list) and if you consider your environment to be a reflection of you and your personality is that honestly how you want to feel? See how we're right back to the self care thing again?

- Do you make your bed every morning or do you leap up, ignore it and then fall back into it at night without any delicious feeling of that freshly made bed situation you get in every hotel you've dreamed of?
- Do you clean your make up brushes regularly so that they are hygienic and also giving you the best possible application on your skin?
- Do you lay out your clothes the night before so you have less decisions to make in the morning and you can shower, dress and enjoy more time before you dash off?
- Are you taking full responsibility for all the laundry and the housework or is there another grown up in the house that can help lessen the load for you?
- Do you have a huge pile of odd socks that make you want to scream?

I could go on and on with this list of things but I think you get the point. Life starts out simple and then it gets more chaotic the busier we get, and the more people who live with us (whether it's kids, partners, etc).

Try and take some time this week to take a step back. Imagine you were putting your house up for sale and think whether the agent could feasibly come round and take pictures. It's likely that it's not really ready for that … and this isn't about what others will think… it's about what you've settled for. Are you happy with things like this or do they need a bit of a change?   What can you do, that's simple, that will make things better for you?

- Can you hire a cleaner?
- Can you do one 5 minute job whilst your toast is on in the morning (polish a mirror or whip round with the hoover).
- Can you declutter? This takes longer than you think but boy, is it cathartic! You will feel lighter emotionally and physically for getting rid of stuff you don't need. Look up Marie Condo if you haven't come across her before and find yourself in a world of joy!
- Can you carve some space, just for you, where you can put your laptop, some pens and a pad, and create a tranquil space for you to think and work? If space is tight you can get flip-up tables from Ikea that are super for this type of thing. Use your imagination!
- Can you speak to your partner and come up with a rota of jobs so it's not all on your shoulders?

Write down here the thing that bugs you most about your environment:

Write down here the things you're going to do to tackle it:

- Set up a command centre in your hallway so that keys/bags/shoes can be quickly stored and quickly grabbed.
- Book a weekend in your diary to declutter as much as you possibly can.
- Give your laptop an overhaul - empty the 'bin', update your screensaver to something worth looking at and change your password to something motivational.
- Clean your windows. Yes - seeing the outdoors more clearly does make a difference!

Now remember environment doesn't just mean physical space. It can also mean people.

As an entrepreneur/business owner it's really important to protect your mindset and if you're surrounded with negative nellies or time-vampires it can make the task so much harder. I appreciate that you can't just make your family disappear (although I know it would be nice sometimes!) but what you can do is take yourself off to a coffee shop or set aside some regular time to work on your business where the door is shut and you cannot be disturbed. If you have an understanding partner then get them involved.

Take a look at who you are connected to online. If you're seeing posts from people that make you feel down in the dumps or any other negative type of emotion then remove them from your feed, or disconnect from them completely or simply silence them.

Stop watching the news. This is something which I did many many years ago now and one which the late Richard Denny (author of Selling to Win) shared with me that he also did. I remember taking tea with him at his home a few years back and he said to me, "Coralie, I don't get the papers any more because it's just a distraction and most of it is just miserable". After all, most of what is pumped at you is negative, generally spun and leaves you feeling helpless. Instead, concentrate on your local community and close contacts and vow to make a difference there. I imagine if we all did that then the world would probably be a different place. You can't generally impact what happens across the globe and in fairness if the news is important you'll find out about it soon

Your life is going on
Tik Tok, Tik Tok

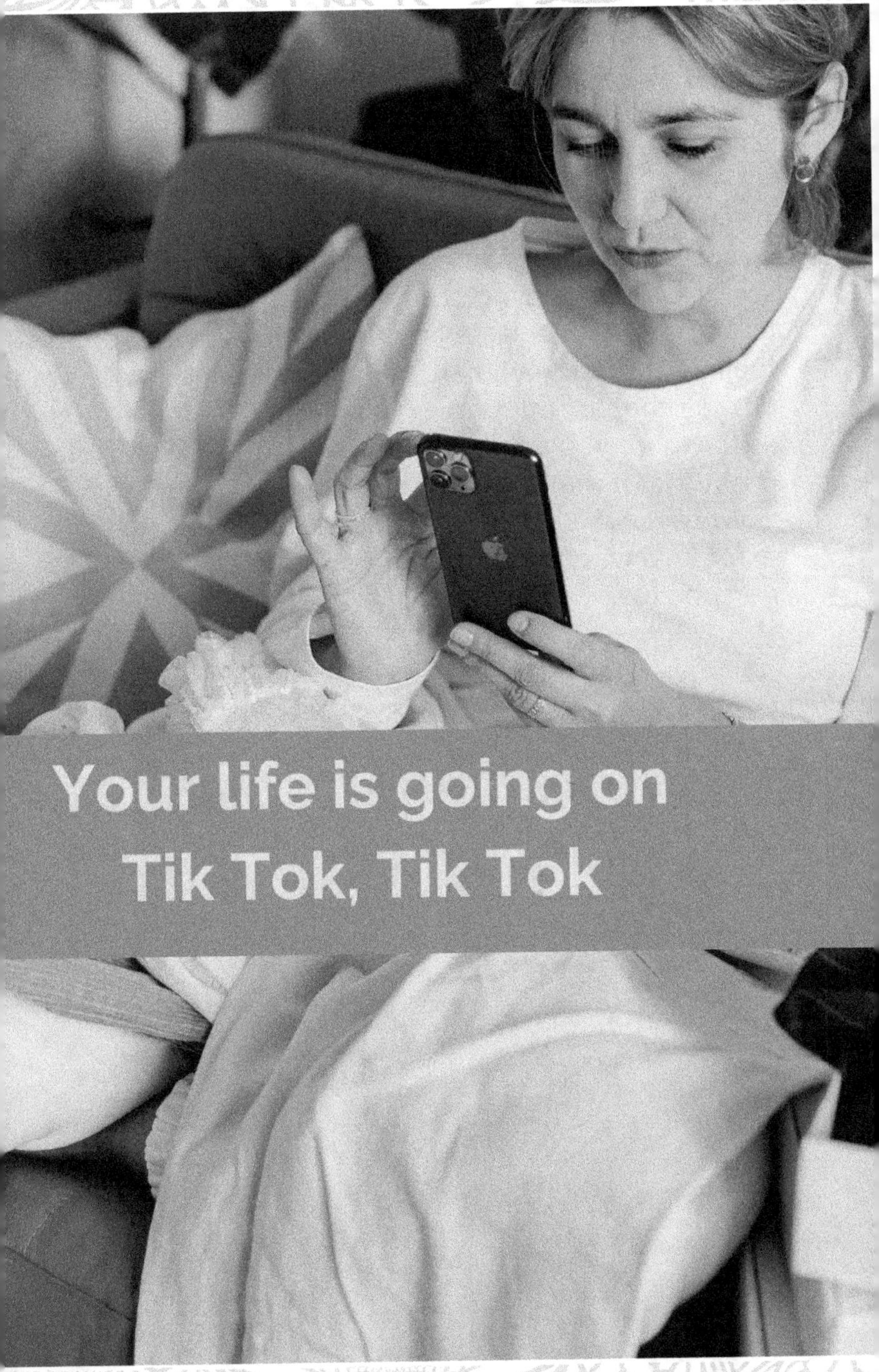

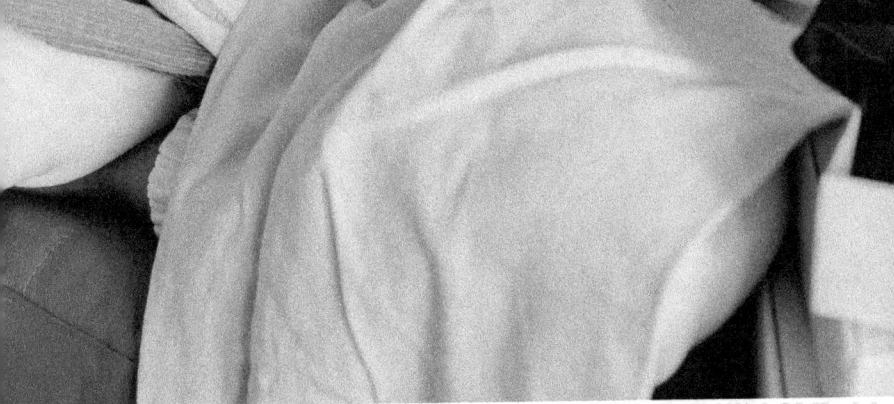

enough. Turn off the news apps from your phone and focus on your lane. In my opinion the news environment is not one that you want to be living in.

Lastly take a look at what media you are consuming. Are you reading and listening to things that motivate/educate/inspire or relax you? Or are you mindlessly scrolling or absorbing content which is of either no value or negative value (in other words leaves you feeling as though you are somehow lacking in one way or the other?). Your phone will give you some insights as to where you are spending your time. (Tip - TikTok is not a pastime).

Write down what you can do to improve your external environment from a people/media perspective:

Chapter 5 Review and Actions - Environment dictates performance

- Look at where you're working. Do you have dedicated space that makes you feel good and is practical?
- Have a think about what you can do to make things better.
- Write down what bugs you about your environment.
- .. and what you can do to tackle it.
- Disconnect from people online and in real life who bring you down or draw energy from you that leaves you feeling less than yourself.
- Stop watching the news! (Or at the very least don't do it before you go to bed!)
- Write down what you can do to improve your environment from a people/media perspective.

Chapter 6. Know your Numbers

We have talked so far about clearing the decks so that you can focus on you and your business and removing fear so that you can succeed. So now it's time to double down and get real about where you are with things.

One thing I've learned is that by not having a good understanding of the numbers in your business you are certainly going to have an issue crop up quite quickly. No matter how much passion you have, knowledge and training you've done, or volume of customers held on your books, if you don't know the numbers which are underpinning your business you will, inevitably fall over. Either through making an uninformed decision, through not drawing enough money to sustain your home or though overcommitting to purchasing equipment/resources and then becoming insolvent. Many business owners focus their time on forging ahead and 'doing' the job at the expense of working 'on their business'. I can only liken it to getting into a self driving car with no map or instructions and hoping you're going to end up at the right place at the right time with no accidents on the way.

Many of us kid ourselves that we don't need to do this work. We either delegate it out to book keepers and accountants, or someone else in the business because we're 'not good at numbers' or we fall for the belief that we shouldn't do stuff we don't like or are not good at. But please believe me that this is the one bit of your business you really need a handle on. I'm not suggesting that you become a book keeper, or you try and do your own accounts. There is a very distinct difference. We employ others who are qualified and trained in this area to make sure that the financials are presented in a certain way to make you legally compliant and so that you pay the correct amount of taxes. They can churn out management reports and forecasting for you if you pay them to, and these things can be useful if you actually understand the numbers that you're looking at. But for the most part, what I'm advocating for here is that you take responsibility and ownership for what is happening in your business, day to day, so that you can let the professionals neatly wrap those numbers up for you whilst you do something else.

So what are the actual numbers that I'm talking about?

Let me tell you a story.

There was a lady called Rachel (names and details have been changed to protect the innocent here!) who ran a very successful salon. She had built it up over a few years and was relying very much on a full column and word of mouth for her business. Her days were busy, she was stood on her feet for many hours a day and she liked nothing more than a large glass of rose in the evening before she rolled back in again the next day to do it all again. Rachel hadn't had one of those 'oh sh*t' moments in her business because, up to this point, things had been going pretty well.

What's an 'oh sh*t' moment I hear you ask? In fairness they're anything that makes you feel slightly sick, wobbled or gives you that face-plant feeling enough to stop you concentrating on the work ahead. It could be an HMRC notification of your tax bill, a complaint from a customer all over social media, a sudden and massive increase in material costs …. Basically anything that was probably unexpected and smacks you back into the reality that unless you've stuffed some good money into the bank the stability of your business is probably only as good as the last days takings.

Rachel is typical of many business owners where, when things are great, they're great. But when they're not they can implode your mental health and your ability to fix a problem.

And it is generally finances or staff who will have the biggest 'oh sh*t' impact on your business. I guarantee when one of these happens everybody goes through a few phases. Phase 1 - feeling sick and anxious. Phase 2 - starting to work out what has happened and/or going into utter denial and looping back to Phase 1, and Phase 3 (for those of us with staying power) - getting on with sorting it out.

Imagine if you will that Rachel was out with her daughter one weekend and slipped and fell whilst ice-skating. She sprained her wrist which meant she couldn't see clients for the first time in 3 years. She had just taken on an expensive lease for a tanning machine and was relying on an increase in her prices to cover the initial months costs whilst the demand increased. But now Rachel can't work. Her insurance doesn't cover everything needed to keep the business afloat. And she has enjoyed a few weeks of shopping through her business account to buy stuff from PLT and

BooHoo ready for her annual vacation to Mexico. After all, she has worked really hard for it so why not take the money out? She'd already drawn her basic salary but wanted a bonus because she'd been back to back for weeks and deserved the treats. So the business should be paying for those things, of course....

And so, with that slip on the ice, she begins that moment of 'oh sh*t' because she doesn't really know what she's going to do. She doesn't have full sight of her business finances because there has always been enough each month to cover everything and if she needs more she just books in a few more clients. But now she can't. And suddenly those extra purchases from PLT and BooHoo become resented, the salon becomes a noose around her neck and the thought of what will happen before the next VAT return makes her feel sick.

Sounding familiar? I have done this exercise with many business owners and I'd like you to do it too. Right now. Put your big girl pants on and lets go.

Getting back control

Print out the last 3 months of your business bank statements. Make sure you do this for all accounts if you have more than one. Don't skip this bit if you think 'oh it's fine, my accountant does all this'. Trust me, it's important.

Now, grab some coloured pens. The idea is that you are going to go through this bank statement, line by line and categorise your spending. It's up to you how you choose to do this but the following ideas might help you:

- Stationery, supplies and other smaller overheads
- Rent and utilities (eg: water, broadband, heating etc)
- Business rates and other taxes
- Materials (genuinely things you've bought to create the 'thing' your business does rather than the 'fake' stuff you try and shove through for tax reasons)
- Capital expenditure/equipment lease etc
- Personal expenses. This one is the kicker. How many Uber eats are you putting through the business because you can't be arsed to make a packed lunch? How many new outfits are you buying with the 'excuse' that they are tax deductible even though we both know another Zara handbag is not a business necessity? How many food shops are going through your business account? Have you got subscriptions you don't actually need?

You get the idea.
Now add up each category.
Are you happy with the totals?
If not, remove what isn't needed and see what improvements you can make.
Monitor each category each month and see if they stay reasonably static.
It's easy to skip by this stuff but what isn't easy (probably) is the effort and sacrifice you've made to earn the money in the first place. How many hours have you put in making or doing / chasing down invoices / getting up early just to blow it all with a quick online purchase when the money hits the bank? I have taught this concept to countless business owners, all of whom without fail have found nuggets of gold

within their businesses. From the gut-churning realisation of money being poured down the drain in unused subscriptions, to being far stricter with personal spending, I have literally saved thousands and thousands each year simply by following easy steps that anyone can do. If you'd like to explore this further then follow me at @themamabearceo on Instagram where you can grab all of this from me via a bite-sized course .

    I guarantee if you did as our grandparents taught us, which is be careful with every penny, you'd have more of a buffer in your account to get you through a few weeks of no work like Rachel. I also guarantee the majority of us are kidding ourselves when we think how well we're doing financially. Turnover isn't impressive. How much money you are bringing into your house WHILST LEAVING YOUR BUSINESS ACCOUNT HEALTHY is impressive. Stripping your business to create a lifestyle at home that isn't sustainable without a cash cow behind it is just creating a false reality that will blow down like the house in the three little piggies the moment the wind changes direction. No, you don't need a Porsche on lease. No, you don't need a posh premises. No, you don't need half of the stuff you think you do. Not until you can actually pay for it outright. Trust me. You'll sleep better, your business will work better and your future self will thank you.

    What else can you do?

    So you've been pretty good, you've checked your bank statements and actually the figures are looking pretty healthy. You might want to have another look at what you're paying for stock and materials and see if there are any savings to be made. When did you last look at your prices? Do they reflect the service you're providing? Remember, you can afford to put your prices up and there will be a certain amount of customers you lose without seeing a difference on your bottom line. Less effort, same or more money.

(Side note though, greed isn't attractive. Fair pricing and honesty is.)

Have a look at what you are paying yourself. Is it enough? Do you need to make adjustments to your household budget to enable you to stress less about how much you need to earn? It's important to take a regular payment so that you feel energised in your business and know that all of your needs are met. After all, I've said it loads of times but if you don't pay yourself then you've just got a very expensive and time consuming hobby. Set yourself a target when you just start out to pay yourself something, even if it's just a small amount, on a fixed date, each month. Good habits like this will take you far.

Now lets move onto Mama Bear's CEO KPI's.

What I want you to do next, once you've checked your statements, is to mark in your diary a time each month where you'll go through your bank and reconcile every line, just like you've already done, so that you know exactly what's happening in your account.

Then set up a small list of things you want to track. As CEO of your business you want to know how well things are going, right? Remember, most people ignore these things because it's easier to abdicate the complicated stuff or stuff you'd rather not think about to somebody else. But it doesn't make the things go away. It just removes your thoughts from them. What it doesn't do is remove your responsibility.

Face up to the fact that the numbers are the heartbeat of your business. YOUR BUSINESS. The thing you spawned, poured all your time into and the thing you intend to make money from. It's not going to drive itself. So start manifesting your dreams and focus on the numbers!

Of course it's totally up to you what you want to track. Nobody else can tell you what is or isn't important. But for now let me give you a few starters for 10 and you can create your own list. Make sure, before you choose something to track, that you're actually able to get the data needed to follow those numbers. Sometimes it can be more time consuming to track a trend in something than it is doing anything about that particular number so be mindful what you choose. (By the way, if you're not sure what a KPI is it stands for Key Performance Indicator and it's just a fancy way of saying it's an important thing of your choice that you want to focus on to see how well your business is doing. For example, if you were following a strict diet, a set of KPI's would probably include your weight, blood pressure and bodily measurements. You start by recording where you are right now, set a target and then track how you're going each week or month).

Where the focus goes, you'll get growth.

You might like to start with the following monthly figures:

* Revenue. Net figures only. If you're VAT registered then the VAT element doesn't need to be part of this - if you feel like you need to include these numbers when looking at your business then go and give your ego a talking to in the mirror. Being an official collector of taxes does not elevate you to greater importance. Having a healthy profit margin is waaaaay more impressive. Turnover is vanity and profit is sanity!
* Costs. Again, look at what is physically coming out of your bank and you can categorise these to see if there are any fluctuations that you want to track.
* Your pay.
* Staffing (including training and onboarding costs)
* Active customers
* Leads - your total pool
* Leads - warm
* Prospects - those who are booked for consultations
* Google reviews / customer satisfaction score

Now, once you start to set goals for your business you may find you want to add more/different things to this list so that you can track the effectiveness of your actions on your business. But it's better to just have a small set of metrics that you do, religiously and consistently, than it is to have an impressive list in January and nothing recorded by December.

A useful tip I was given once was to focus on one needle moving activity each quarter. So instead of having a set of goals such as 'increase customers by 10%, increase revenue by 10% and pull in another 20 leads a week' you're better off picking just one of these and concentrate on that ONE THING for a quarter. This allows you to fully brainstorm and invest in a strategy and know whether it is working or not, instead of scatter-gunning your energy into multiple tactics. You'll still record the data for the others but using this method you'll see how focusing on one strategy affects the results of each KPI.

Allowing yourself to deep dive on one metric gives you the time and opportunity to be able to brainstorm many, many ideas around how to make improvements rather than only partially work on it because you've got another three to manage. Think about it like having kids. If you've only got one it's way easier to help them with their homework than it is when you have four. But if you were able to do them in rotation then you'd spend better quality time tackling the issue than just brushing over it before you move to the next one.

Also, before you decide on your set of KPI's you might want to have in front of you your overall business goal. Not sure what that actually is yet? Write it down here!

Then once you know your overall goal, your KPIs can be in alignment with that.

For example, your overall business goal could be something along the lines of 'Create a business that allows me to earn £5k per month, providing an employment opportunity to one person and for me to become the local go-to expert on xyz.'

Creating KPIs that help meet that goal would look something like this.

You'd monitor your revenue each month as well as your profit. You'd start tracking your earnings each month and also your monthly sales. It would be

our business numbers are YOUR RESPONSIBILITY

important to understand how many people come to you by way of a referral (after all, if you're the expert then people will recommend you) and you'd want to know your profit margins to see if you are able to take on a staff member.

Against each of these indicators, you'll need to decide what the target is. So for example you may say that by the end of the quarter your earnings need to increase by £200 and in order to do that you're going to want to agree a strategy. And that's where, by choosing only one of these to focus on for a whole quarter, you can come up with a whole raft of ideas to hit the target rather than just one or two.

Jot down here the areas that you'd like to focus more on (remembering the old adage that things grow where the focus goes)....

Chapter 6 Review and Actions - Know your numbers

- You need to understand these to stop future failures in your business. Abdicating responsibility to another person or outsourced accountant because 'they do numbers' is zero excuse for not having an understanding of what is happening inside your business
- Print out the last three months bank statements.
- Set up categories for your spending and allocate a colour to each one.
- Go through every line of each statement and categorise it
- Add up your spending in each category.
- Mark time in your diary monthly to repeat this exercise with the previous month's statement
- Paying yourself properly whilst not stripping your business is impressive.
- Look at what you're paying yourself. Is it enough?
- Buying things you can't afford whilst running your business to make it 'look' more impressive will bring it all crashing down.
- Visit @themamabearceo on Instagram and I'll walk you through this exercise, step by step.
- Set up your KPI's and align them with your overall business goal.
- Write them down and focus on one.

Chapter 7. Is it all too much?

Now that you've done a deep dive into your numbers, come up from behind the sofa to look into the bank account and set up some KPIs for yourself, you may be feeling a bit of excitement about where all of this could lead.

If it's sent you into a blind panic then take a breather for a bit. None of this is worth affecting your health over, and if business is stopping you from sleeping you need to take some action now to get back to a place of calm. Lack of sleep impacts your immunity, weight, mood and so much else that it isn't worth getting into the spiral of exhaustion. Do yoga, journal, get some fresh air… whatever it takes to help you keep a healthy perspective on work. And trust me, I've got the T'shirt (plus an entire matching wardrobe) on this subject. Here are a few tips that I've previously used to help get me through some of the harder times.

* Rate the 'thing' that is giving you stress from 1-10 with 10 being the 'worst thing ever'. OK, if I now said you were going to drop dead next week, would this thing still be worthy of the rating? You'll find that 99% of things suddenly become utterly irrelevant faced with this fact. Now, the reality is that

I hope you're not going to drop dead next week, but the point is, a day will come when you do. Do you actually think that all these things which you've allowed to enter your head and settle in, making noise and taking over your precious calm, deserve to stay in there, uninvited? Do you think, in your last moments, that the pissy email you've had from Deidre in accounts payable was actually worth spending a day or so getting heart palpitations over? Or would you have been better looking at the email, taking some time to work out why it's bothered you so much, and then deal with it and move on? I'm simplifying but in fairness life must remain simple in order to protect oneself from too much stress. What's the 'big thing' right now?

* Remember that all you have right now, is now. There are many books on this subject that you can read, to remind yourself that what has gone is done. Finished. You cannot change it and going round it in your head doesn't change it. (That being said, if you have PTSD please seek the help of a counsellor because oftentimes your brain will continue to go

over a scenario to try and find a different outcome and these conditions often need professional assistance). For those situations where we keep pressing 'repeat' because we either want to beat ourselves up, or think we can undo something that has happened, you can't. Stop it. Focus on now. Take a breath. Because now is literally all we have. The future isn't real and hasn't yet happened and you can ruin the next 'now' moment by worrying and upsetting yourself over what has been and gone. If you haven't read The Power of Now by Eckhart Tolle then do grab yourself a copy and he'll explain it all far more eloquently than I! Have a think about all the things that you have, right now, for which you are grateful.

* Imagine your business idol, or someone very successful. Imagine they were presented with the same issue that you're dealing with. How do you think they'd react? What would their advice be to you?

- Do you think that you're the only one to deal with this problem? It's OK to share your thoughts with your close network because this does not make you vulnerable. It makes you human. Everyone in business has issues, every day, that they need to tackle. That's where the strongest survive. Make sure you have people around you who understand what you're doing that you can confide in. Think about people you'd like to get to know better, or indeed meet. Think about how you might get in touch with them and how you can also contribute positively to their world.

- Decide how much energy and time you want to give up to this issue or problem based on how much time and energy you actually have to give. Is it worth taking this away from the things that you

WANT to give time and energy to? If not, deal with it quickly and move on.

- Go out into nature. If you can, wander about barefoot. Find your balance and perspective in the woods, or by the water. Forest bathing, cold water swimming and just a good old walk can pay dividends for your physical and mental health.

- Confront the problem head on. Don't hide from it, hope it will go away or distract yourself. Make it the first thing you deal with (eat the frog). You'll most likely feel a lot better once it is done. It's a bit like going to an interview and having to wait 20 minutes for your appointment. You end up sitting in the waiting room and getting nervous, second guessing what you'll be asked, judging yourself against the other candidates in the room and before you know it you've got yourself in a right state in your head, with sweaty palms and butterflies in your stomach. Now imagine turning up, walking straight in and shaking hands with the interviewer. You get stuck straight into conversation, your nerves don't really have a chance to take hold and you are confident and in your stride. That's a much better mindset and position to take, right? So do that with your problems. Don't leave them festering with you in the waiting room of purgatory.

* And if you're feeling really petrified by the thought of the problems, just pick one or two 'low hangers' and do those first to get you started and feeling strong.

Now, how much do you actually want?

Use the next page to be honest and brainstorm how much you want in your personal and business life....

I have mentored and coached many business owners who are of the belief that they must grow. That constantly striving for 'more' is the only measure of success. That they must market-dominate, be the leader and push harder every day to achieve ever extending goals. These pressures are often cloaked in a cape of fear, with feelings like 'well if I don't take on staff, how will I cope?', 'my competitor has a bigger ad presence on Facebook', 'I'm not filling my books to capacity', 'I should have a bricks and mortar presence', and other such sleep-reducing thoughts.

There are occasions when all of these thoughts are valid. If you want to make millions, if you want to be the market leader, if you want to smash everyone else out of the park then yes, you need to be all-in, with no distractions and it's likely your entire life will be focussed in work.

But for others, this is not the path to success. If you don't believe me then at this point I want you to dive out for a moment and read the book 'Company of One' by Paul Jarvis. This whole book will reassure you that it is perfectly OK to have a successful business without the need for massive staffing, overheads or pressure.

Let me reassure you too. When I worked as a software provider to independent publishers I was fortunate to be in a position to both consult and mentor some very, very successful businesses. They were making profit margins far greater than the 'big glossies', and mostly from their kitchen tables. They had bigger circulations, were making more money and had less stress. Why?

In a nutshell, they were targeting a niche market, in a consistent way doing a job that was possible from a garden office (or in many cases a kitchen table). They knew the method to make the money and were satisfied with a very varied job that they could happily fit around their kids. Amusingly, when we launched our software, many of these 'wife-led' businesses became 'couple-led' businesses because the dashboard we created suddenly gave serious credibility to the monthly revenue and profit and husbands and partners realised they could leave the commute and dive in to help. I was privileged to be able to assist these businesses in their success by delivering systems to help them and I was delighted to watch them grow simply through streamlining processes that ordinarily took them forever manually (eg: invoicing went down to about 20 seconds from a 1-2 day job).

For the ones that wanted to become 7 figure businesses there was an element of staffing that was needed, sometimes premises (but not always) and of course sheer hard work.

Their turnover was impressive and their reader reach was equally great. BUT I don't think that any of their founders actually reached the tipping point where their personal earnings were significantly greater than when they were doing it on a smaller scale. Don't fall into the trap of creating an impressive turnover by trading your sanity and life for longer hours, greater overheads and more mouths to feed to essentially keep your personal income static.

Unless you can calculate an increase in personal income and believe it is worthwhile and achievable then I urge you to sit down and assess why you want to take on premises/staff/etc.

If you:
- Have a customer base that repeatedly purchases
- Are drawing a wage that allows you to put some aside for a rainy day
- Enjoy what you do
- Know how to generate new leads
- Cover your overheads

Then ask yourself these questions:
- What would the benefit be of 'more'?
- Am I prepared to do the work to get it?
- Do I want to make the sacrifices to get it?
- For whose benefit would I be making this effort?
- Is this really what I want?
- When I get to the point of having 'more' what will that do for my life/family/mental health?

Many of the business owners I know who have grown in order to take more market share are working harder with more stresses and yet don't actually earn any more money. So the knock-on effect in their lives is not positive. They are at home less, have less time to do the activities that they wanted to do when they became self employed in the first place, have poorer health (mental and physical) and don't have the extra money to spend on items to support their greater workload such as cleaners, massage therapists etc.

And when asked, many of them wonder why they didn't just stay as they were to begin with.

And that, really, is the point of this chapter. You have to be really sure what your end goals are before randomly commencing on a growth journey. Don't be sucked in by all the business 'gurus' that tell you to keep pushing and growing when you're not sure that's aligned with your principle reason for running your own business. Define what growth actually means for you because it doesn't just mean working more hours. Remember, you can increase profit simply by upping your prices (although I'm being simplistic here of course). It doesn't just mean that you have to get more customers and work harder. There are other ways of doing things without the '90's style hustle and push that many of us have been brought up to believe is the only way.

This is probably the right time to insert an article I wrote for a magazine which explains this in the context of my life and why I'm so passionate about it now:

Slow down and see the world

My life used to be run at a hundred miles an hour. I got pregnant at 23 with my first daughter and found myself in a society that was pushing the 'you can have it all' lifestyle, complete with shoulder pads and Chanel handbag. As a result, needing to work was almost an inbuilt requirement and as a new mum I had to work even harder to demonstrate that I was capable – going back full time with a 12 week old baby was no mean feat and I have no idea how I managed.

Set goals so big they laugh. Crush them while they watch.

Pumping milk and storing it in the work fridge during lunchtimes, panicking at a leaky boob when sitting in the boardroom, endless, endless driving from home to childminders to work to home and doing it all again the next day....

'Overdoing it' became my normal. I continued to work long hours in a corporate job and juggled school runs and after school clubs with conference calls and flights to various countries. I squeezed in cooking where I could, coffees with my friends on occasion but most of the time I was pushing my mind and body way harder than I ever should (now I look back) in an effort to keep up with a 'normal' lifestyle. wasn't lavish, I didn't have a massive house but to not have financial stress every month and to be able to keep the bills paid I needed to work really hard. Two more children later my body, and mind started to show signs of struggle. I had a few episodes of depression. Looking back I was developing auto-immune issues. I had constant low-grade infections. But I still kept pushing because, frankly, I didn't know how else to be. Trying to slow my brain down felt utterly impossible and to my cortisol-fuelled nervous system whenever I tried to slow down, panic would set in as though the world was about to end.

MI simply didn't believe that living slower, with less pressure, would set me up with a life of safety and fulfilment. Don't get me wrong, I have ALWAYS appreciated the little things. A good cup of tea, reading, sunshine and hand-written letters. Listening to the birds singing and snuggles on the sofa. But these things were always lower down in my priority list and snatched in between moments of writing project plans, system specifications, staffing reports and then later compiling and editing magazines.

I am a big believer in that where you are right now is exactly where you're meant to be based on the choices you've made and the universe always knowing best. And now, I can honestly say I've never been happier. I have a little more time to really do more of the things that make me smile. Even yesterday we were pottering about the garden and we discovered a little set of solar lights that had been covered up. With a quick clean and a rearrange we were thrilled to see a splash of colour appear over the Spanish BBQ that came with our new garden. It looked like an old-fashioned Christmas tree and it cost us nothing, other than a little bit of effort. It would have been easier to have chucked them in the bin but because I'm not dashing to yet another meeting I was able to spend a minute enjoying the possibility of resurrecting something.

With the rising cost of living now becoming almost unsustainable for many of us, and businesses having to increase all their prices and, by default, being shoved into the VAT threshold, I feel like we are being spun back into the world I have left and no longer want to go back to. We are having to work harder and harder - the government answer to everything is 'earn more' and 'suck it up'. My view is different. Forget what everyone else is doing. Every day of your life is yours to enjoy and if all you're doing is running around to cover the bills then that's not life. Reconsider your expectations of what you want to consume - whether it's clothing, home accessories or even media. Do you really need all those things? I only have one toilet to clean now instead of six and I can tell you that small thing is worth a quick wait whilst someone else is using it!

There's nothing wrong with having less and doing less and it honestly doesn't matter what anyone else thinks. If planning rules weren't so ridiculous in this country I would go and buy a small bit of land and plonk a cabin on it now, create a lovely big garden, have chickens and forget what instagram thinks I should have. Because by slowing down, I'm seeing way more of the world, and that to me is priceless.

I've been that person who has pushed and hustled. And don't get me wrong, there is always a time and a place in your employment/work journey where that is absolutely appropriate. But if you're having to go the extra mile every single day, if your dreams don't come to fruition, or your health suffers as a result, was it really worth it? Slogging yourself is not a pre-requisite to success. And when I see people following in my footsteps I want to shout a loud mama-bear 'stooooooooop!'

Because I can see a little bit further down the road and what's coming isn't generally what you think is there. Burnout and dissatisfaction are very real unless you sort out your priorities from the get-go. And for many of us we don't take the time to do that because we're often young enough to push on through and naive enough to think everything will be ok. Then chuck in a whole load of Instagram/TikTok/social media 'reality' where you end up believing you're an utter failure unless you can live a laptop lifestyle making squillions with your big toe, stood next to a Lambo and surrounding yourself with 'stuff' to prove your worth.

Sod that. I'd rather grow veggies in my garden and have time to sit in the sun and read (or write) a damn good book. I don't give a crap what other people think I should be doing with my life and I'll bet my other big toe that on their deathbeds they'd wished they'd taken better care of themselves and/or their loved ones instead of working 100 hours a week to make a monthly car payment.

So think about it again. What is it that you really, truly want? Imagine your perfect day and write it down here:

Chapter 7 Review and Actions - Is it all too much?

- It's Ok to take a breather. Think about what is stressing you and rate these things from 1-10.
- Think about what you're grateful for.
- What advice would you get from your business idol for the problems you are facing right now?
- Who's in your support network?
- Decide what needs sorting and how much energy you're prepared to put into those things
- Go out into nature. Do this every day!
- Deal with the issues that are building up inside your head. Pick one or two low hangers and get them sorted.
- Brainstorm how much you actually want in your personal and business life and define what growth actually means to you.
- Create your perfect day.

Chapter 8. Are you bubbling in perturbation?

As a self confessed control freak, disguised as a bloody good Project Manager, I feel very qualified to teach on this subject. I used to want everything to be close to perfect until I realised this stemmed from my self worth and confidence rather than what was actually needed. So over the years I've learned to balance, as best I can, what should be close to perfect and what will be good enough. Having a family of 5 kids plus various animals in the mix helps you do this rather well and you learn great strategies to help you cope when you're running a busy house - just like a busy business. Bulk buying boxer shorts and socks in the same colour for the boys so there was no need to worry whose was whose. Having a command centre in the hallway for book bags and shoes so that coming to and from school was always easy. Keeping a digital and printed copy of my diary so I never forgot rosters and meetings. Having a weekly food plan so I only had to think once about what we were going to cook instead of having a daily headache… you get the idea. Deploying coping mechanisms and organisational strategies is imperative if you are to get through mostly unscathed and with some level of success. But equally, knowing when to skid in by the skin of your teeth because you've packed out the day with important things is OK too. We are not living our lives on Instagram and if you haven't hoovered the living room in two weeks don't worry too much (just don't leave it much longer than that or it will take up space in the to-do list in your head!).

Anyway, I digress.

The point I'm making is that when you start a business it's often with the intention of wanting everything to be perfect. You've thought through all the scenarios, you've ordered your stock, bought the website, picked the colours… and then the work actually starts and before you know it you are literally rushed off your feet trying to IMPLEMENT. And this is where many of us fall flat on our faces because having multiple balls in the air is really hard, especially if you don't want them to come down.

Oftentimes, at the start of a new business it's just you. So you spend your day in 'front of house' (wherever that may be) and before you know it you're multitasking, grabbing different hats from book-keeping to web building, customer care to CRMs and you haven't had time to spend actually doing the actual thing you went into business to do! Or, you are so busy doing the thing you should be doing that the other hats never get put on and it starts crumbling behind you in an epic-adventure-movie-style disaster.

So you spin around, mop up the chaos behind you, and then turn around to do the same again and before you know it you're running around like a headless chicken wondering what on earth you're doing thinking you can run a business, not to mention have some sort of life as well, and it all starts to become a bit much.

In fairness, this is normal and most of us have to go through a bit of this to pop out the other side. It is when it is at its most chaotic that you need to remember self care because chances are you'll forget to drink the water, get the fresh air, sleep and eat healthy food, which will push you into a downward spiral where you're simply not up to the job. Now's the time to double down on these things because it will make you better equipped to manage the chaos.

This sense of perturbation is not pleasant, and not a place that you want to stay in for very long. Imagine it being like a pan of water on the hob. You turn up the temperature and it starts to bubble. The water is being agitated inside the pan. At this point you can either choose to turn the temperature up and let it boil, turning it to steam, or you can turn the temperature down so it stops bubbling. What you don't want to do is leave it so it just stays being agitated. When you and your business are in this state it's very hard, unhealthy and ultimately you have to make the choice of which way you want to push - will you turn up the temperature and break through or will you turn it down and retract?

Depending on the circumstances, there are no right or wrong answers. But what is important is that some things during this process do not get missed. And those are the detailed bits that can make a good business amazing. It's the little things that made you stand out, that you may think are superfluous but actually go to the heart of what you do.

   Think about places or service based businesses where you go time and again and then think about why you do that. It's generally because of good service and treatment. My partner paid for a one hour massage for me for my birthday one year. I was so excited (I really needed it!) and couldn't wait to lay down on the massage couch, with the lighting soft and the gentle music to lull me into a peaceful world of no interruptions, all for me for a whole hour. For the first 10 minutes the music on the sound system kept stalling which jolted me out of my blissed-out state and flung me back into my head (the to-do list reappeared pretty quickly) and my annoyance levels started heightening when nothing was done to sort it.

   I was told that the 'Wi-Fi was a bit dodgy' that day and so they switched it off and for the remaining 45 minutes the room was silent. There was no chilled out bliss for me, just a rather uncomfortable awareness of someone else breathing and attempting a full body massage in a very quiet situation. So on leaving, I let Sean know what had happened and rightly so he mentioned it when he settled the bill. There was no offer of another massage, no free drinks in the bar for my birthday to make up for the disappointment... literally nothing. Interestingly this establishment went into administration last week.

   Always a shame when a business fails but I very much hope any new owner has a backup for their systems when they fail. It wouldn't have been difficult to have had a backup for music in the cupboard - even if it was an old iPhone connected via Bluetooth to a speaker just for an eventuality like this. If you are offering a service that has component parts (so in this case it was massage lotions, a member of staff, music and a couch) you need to be sure that if one of those things doesn't work/isn't available you have a backup so that you can still offer the service. It's a bit like home grocery shopping - the supermarket will offer you an alternative if there is something unavailable and if they pick well you're likely to keep it and not feel too much disappointment for the thing you didn't get. You'll feel pleased that the store have tried to rectify things and offer something else, instead of just saying 'no'.

So in your own business, think about the non-negotiable details that set you apart. From the way the telephone is answered to the way that you wrap a product. Taking time to talk to your customers so that they truly feel heard, sending them welcome gifts or making sure that you regularly check in with them. Whatever it is that you choose, make sure you are in a position to continue doing those things because that is what your customers will be coming back for. Everything in life is about how you make someone feel. It's about the experience and the feelings. Watching your new shoes being carefully wrapped in crisp tissue paper before being put back into the box, having a little heart sprinkled on top of your coffee, your towel beautifully laid out for you at the pool, a checklist given to you to help you or a chocolate in an organza bag on the pillows when the house has been cleaned… whatever it is you choose, make it about your customers emotions and keep those feelings high on your importance list because that's what will keep them returning, recommending and reviewing you.

So even if you feel like you're drowning, don't let the important little details slip. Keep your eyes focussed on your customers and the rest will fall into place. Just don't stay on the hob bubbling for too long. Either work out how to be more efficient, get some help or do less. But keep your standards!

Jot down here the things which set you apart, or what you want to offer as part of your business that will become non-negotiable. Make them part of the DNA of your company so that they can't slip.

Chapter 8 Review and Actions - Are you bubbling in Perturbation?

- Do you feel as though you are like a pot on the boil, just simmering and getting no-where, not knowing whether you need to turn up the gas and push on through, or turn the gas down and back off for a bit? What do you need to do to change your state?
- What are the non-negotiable that set your business apart from others?

Chapter 9. It's all about the systems

I love this bit about business and life. Having a diploma in business administration, followed by a career at IBM as an analyst, IT Project Manager and then my own software company I'm pretty clued up on looking at a business and working out the best way to systemise it. I have an uncanny knack for being the middle man between software developers and customers and so I can translate 'tech speak' into 'we can do it like this' language that anyone can understand. As a result I love consulting in companies and taking a global view of their systems, processes and what they're trying to achieve and then poke it about a bit to find out why they're doing what they're doing.

Lets just explore for a moment, the difference between processes and systems. Probably a 'teaching grandma to suck eggs' situation here, but it's important because I think many people muddle the two.

A process is the amalgamation of all the things you need to do in order to make a system work. So for example, you might have a system for social media. Within that system you'll have a series of processes required to make it work. In fact it's likely that you'll have a subset of systems and a subset of processes for many of these things. Using social media as the example, you'll have sub-systems such as Blogs, Video, Posts etc and underneath those you'll have processes that define how each of these systems will run to create an output or end product/goal.

Don't confuse a 'software system' either with a business system. Whilst these may have the same name, they are subtly different. In my mind, a business system is the 'thing', if you like, in which to create processes to achieve that 'thing' such as social media. A software system is simply an online solution to deal with such 'things' and may, or may not deal with multiple 'things'. Whilst in essence the software is a system think of it more as a tool for you to host your systems and processes and be aware that it won't be like a magic wand - you have to do the work to make them work!

It's the systems and processes that help our businesses run and when they are implemented correctly they will save you time, reduce errors, and create a backbone in your company that is robust, allowing you to do what you do best.

Yet oftentimes processes get built so tall that they start to topple like a tower of cards. It all starts off reasonably robust and makes sense but the bigger it grows the less it works until it falls over. And so many businesses make the mistake of over complicating their systems because they think they need to future proof and so purchase unnecessary software etc just because their competitors use it, when in reality they don't understand the systems they're using and only nestle in a corner of them, with the rest being wasted.

Before you opt to purchase any sort of software, whether it's monthly or not, you first need to define what it is you're trying to achieve. Grab a large sheet of paper (the back of a wallpaper roll works brilliantly for this). Write out your main goal at the top and then underneath define the systems you'll need to achieve it.

It could look something like this:

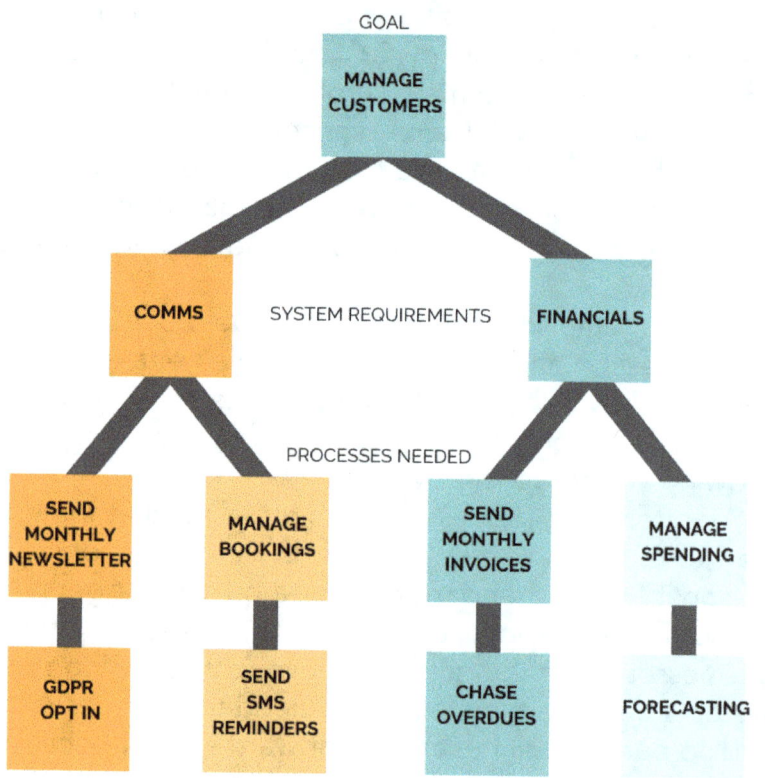

You'll see how from one system, you'll possibly need a few processes to run it. By getting these things down on paper you can see, visually, what is needed. This is a big first step into deciding how to automate and/or move into an online 'system', in other words the actual tools you will use to drive your business. Don't be confused by implementing a 'software system' thinking that has sorted your business out. It hasn't. Do the work first so that you know what it is that you need.

   Create the process manually first. If you can make it make sense on paper then you can translate it easily to software. By physically moving paper around an office (or across your desk) and having paper forms, for example, it's easy to see where the issues or bottlenecks are before you go looking for a system to replicate it.
   Too many times I see business owners distracted by the next shiny thing, they sign up for it, get invested in it and then realise it doesn't do everything they need it to do. So then they try and find another system to do that thing and before they know it they've got a load of different systems that can't speak to each other and a whole load of broken processes. By taking the time to do the manual piece first, even if it is a pain in the butt, you'll have greater success when it comes to automating this in a piece of software.
   So what do you do once you've done the definitions and you're ready to find somewhere to transfer it to?
   Well first of all, digital isn't always best. There are times when good, 'old fashioned' pen and paper will trump an online system purely for its simplicity and cost. This is often dictated by business need.

For example, let's use my daughter as a case study here. She's an award winning, successful hairdresser (probably TMI but it's my book and I'm very proud of her so I can at least blow her trumpet here!). When she first started on her self employment route she had a diary that she used to schedule all her appointments and it worked really well. She was always fully booked and her clients messaged her for availability. This also gave her the opportunity for a 'hi hun, how are you' chat which grew nearly all of them into lifelong customers.

She pencilled them in and then ticked when confirmed. The diary was taken with her when she left the salon so she could continue taking bookings at home and she always knew where her gaps were, simply by opening up the page. Did she need to invest in a system, which would probably come with a monthly overhead, to replace this process? No. Did her customers have problems booking in with her? No. The system worked and it was good enough for her whilst she was building her business.

Roll forward to now and she has a super-salon with several members of employed and self-employed staff and various beauty rooms. Could this be managed on paper? Yes, but the likelihood of a mistake is greater. Also the volume of clients booking is much higher so a software solution to block out the time and send out automatic bookings and reminders became a crucial, time-saving tool. The cost of the overhead far outweighs the potential loss through forgotten bookings or missed appointments so this is a system worth investing in. And most importantly she knew exactly what it was that she needed because she had been running the process already in her paper diary.

Now from an efficiency point of view there are some obvious systems you can employ without the need to fanny about and decide if you need them or not. Every business will need systems to manage the following:

- Customer journey - from lead to onboarding to retention
- Sales - including terms, contracts, method of payment etc
- Operations - including insurances, stock control (or for services allocation of resources), purchasing.
- Finances - including book keeping, accounting, cash forecasting and management of cash itself if applicable
- Marketing - how you're going to reach your market, how you'll retain them, how you'll grow.

And of course there's plenty more. But as you look more closely can you see how many of these are interlinked? How the impact of a marketing strategy may affect the customer journey and how the financial strategy can affect the marketing strategy etc. Which is why, so often, unless these strategies are defined and the processes (the HOW) are written, you end up in a mess such that it looks like a 4 year old's scribble in crayon rather than a clear pathway to a goal.

When you start out you won't necessarily have the foresight to see all of the business requirements ahead of you - experience and time will help you with this - but get someone involved in this session who can help you (unemotionally) map out these systems in a logical way. I love to do this because I can keep pulling my clients back to the purpose of the task rather than drowning in the weeds and complexities (plus I create a mean action list as we're going!).

Once you can see the systems mapped out, with processes detailed underneath, you're in a far better position to then start working out what you need to help streamline and automate your work.

Now, when it comes to choosing your systems, there are factors that you'll need to take into consideration such as:

- cost - will there be monthly or annual charges and if there is a free version will you need to upgrade later (and are the charges ok at that point?)
- Complexity - does it need training and how much of an investment in time or money will it take to implement
- Setting up - will they help you import your data or will you have to do this yourself?
- Does the system comply with UK GDPR regulations?
- Are you able to get support easily either through online chat or phone - there is literally nothing worse than employing a system and not being able to speak to a human if you have any issues.
- Has the system got good reviews?
- Are you able to easily remove your data should you wish to leave - and make sure that there are no large financial penalties for doing this.
- Does the system play nicely with other systems (in other words if you need to integrate one with another is that possible?)

- Are there any options to customise certain fields? For most an off the shelf option is generally the most affordable but some will offer the ability to add some personalisation and specifics. If not see if there is a workaround. Quite often the benefits that a system can bring may outweigh a particular way you want to do things, but you might need to think outside the box.
- Does the system have a good record of uptime (you don't want to be using something that crashes regularly)
- Is your data backed up, fully secure and accessible - in other words does your supplier have robust disaster recovery plans?
- Do you actually like it? Using a system that you enjoy, is aesthetically pleasing AND gets the job done makes for a happier day in my opinion!
- Is the sales website easy to navigate? If they can't build a decent site then it probably says a lot about their own software!
- Is the pricing clear on their site? Chances are, if there is no pricing shown then this is aimed at enterprise (large scale) entities - oftentimes they'll want to book a 'demo' for you. I'd probably steer clear here because you'll be subjected to a sales pitch and then find out the price later. Most likely it will be way out of your ball park and you'll have wasted your time.

Ok, so once you've narrowed down your choice of solutions and picked the software that is right for your business, please take the time to set it up properly from the outset. There is nothing more frustrating than seeing software set up incorrectly, with reports being run that give you the figures for the month, for example, that are skewed with test data or rubbish information because you've spent a few hours playing about and forgetting to delete the stuff that isn't correct. Always remember crap in = crap out so if you want this system to support your business then treat it with respect and remember you're the one driving it, not the other way around!

Bear in mind, too, that unless you have commissioned a bespoke piece of software (which I really don't advocate because there is generally enough off the shelf products to cover most of what you need) there will be an element of adjustment whilst you move from manual to automated.

Whether you import your own data or the software provider does this for you, please, please do checks on the import before you start using the system. Don't blindly assume that everything will be in the right fields. Do random checks on your data set to see if everything is correct. For example, there's nothing worse than sending out an email and adding a 'first name' tag to find that it populates with the first line of their address because one of the cells had shifted in your spreadsheet. It looks tatty and will turn off your customer as fast as a rat up a drainpipe.

Also don't forget the 'bit in the middle'. By this I mean the data that will have accumulated (a bit like belly button fluff) during the time that the import is being done and you starting to use the system. You need to remember to pick it out and add it in before you get started otherwise it will be left behind!

Once you've got underway with your new system I suggest you do the following:

- add diary reminders to your calendar to check, monthly, the reports that may be available in the system. Print them out and check the data. Is it what you're expecting to see? Are there any anomalies in the results? This is one of the advantages of running things manually to start with as you have a benchmark to compare the automated version with.
- If you have other people using the system have a quick check to make sure that they're adding in the data you need (if the field isn't mandatory then it's easy to miss).
- Behave as though you were a recipient of any emails going out, lead pages etc. Fill them in and make sure that what comes back is what you're expecting. This is you, taking care of the customer experience to make sure that everything is working as it should. I'm sure you've already used sites and found links that just don't go anywhere so you get frustrated and go elsewhere. Don't lose business through sloppy system management.
- Ask yourself regularly 'is this system serving me', 'is the cost worth the time saving or sales generated' and just check in with yourself that it is still in alignment with your business goals. Treat the system as though it were a member of staff. It may not have a name but it still needs to perform and do a job for your business. If you feel like it, give it a name and make it a member of staff!

Chapter 9 Review and Actions - It's all about the systems

- Systems and processes are the backbone of a successful company.
- Define what you're trying to achieve and draw out your systems, with the corresponding processes underneath.
- Think about what manual or online tools will satisfy these needs.
- Set up your software/systems and make diary reminders to regularly check the data; re-evaluate if the system is serving you and be a secret shopper to your own systems to make sure they still work!

Chapter 10. Some of my favourite systems

I employ a variety of systems to get me through my work and personal days so I thought I'd share with you what I use, and why.

PAPER SYSTEMS
I've always believed that good, old fashioned pen and paper is generally the best way to manage most things. And for my daily tasks and planning, it's perfect. After all, I spend way too many hours using screens and so being able to turn away and pick up a pen, apply it to paper and use a different part of my brain and hand is incredibly powerful. I like being able to colour code things, arrange things how I like and also turn what is generally quite boring (action lists etc) into something a little more aesthetically pleasing.

So for my work diary I use an A5 Hobonichi cousin. For those of you who are stationery savvy you will probably know how utterly delicious this choice of notebook is simply because of the type of paper employed. To write on Tomoe River paper is nothing short of fabulous because if you use a ball-point and have a reasonably hard pressure the paper ends up slightly crisp and crinkled where you have written.

For those of you less bothered with the aesthetics and more interested in the functionality this is a day to a page diary, dated, with a dot-grid paper and includes both weekly, monthly and yearly planners amongst other things. If you want to find out more about the benefits of the Hobonichi then jump onto Youtube and you will be able to immerse yourself in a whole new world of stationery!

My Hobonichi is on my desk daily and I use it to forward plan. Essentially I have my tasks for the day written in a certain format and at the end of the day anything not done gets moved to the next available slot and everything completed is ticked off and crossed out. Every week I go back a week to be sure there's nothing overlooked and I also cross check my monthly calendar and digital google calendar to ensure I haven't missed any appointments. I have inserted tabs purchased from Etsy to easily jump months in the book and it also has a yummy silicone cover which is clear, that allows me to slide essential planning stickers and other papers inside.

Stationery is life!

For my goal setting planner I use The Daily Grind system. This is a disc-bound system which is super because you can easily add, remove or move pages and the pre-printed set of daily pages is great. They cover a full quarter and allow you to fully plan out your goals, break them down, track them and focus daily on your key 'needle movers' so that slowly but surely you get everything done. Look out for Angie Bellamare on YouTube and you'll find her website on the resources page at the back.

I also journal. I advocate this for all my clients because it is an opportunity to empty your head and reflect on what is good in your world. I have used various systems for journalling and my favourites are:

- A5 undated Stalogy (same paper as Hobonichi - yum!)
- Happy Planners, any size
- Midori travellers notebooks

My journalling style is a mixture of writing and scrap-booking, allowing me to include photographs and other memorabilia. If I'm feeling overwhelmed then a dated journal is useful - it helps me stick to it (I hate missing days) but if you're more regimented then an undated planner is good because you can pick it up and write in it when it matters. That being said, if you are feeling stressed or overwhelmed it's a good idea to do a little bit of journalling at the end of each day and focus on three things you're grateful for.

DIGITAL SYSTEMS

I have used many, many digital systems in my past, either designed by me or off the shelf solutions. It's hard to come up with a definitive list of everything you could use, particularly because we all have different needs and requirements but here are a few of my ongoing favourites which I tend to consistently use in my day-to-day and I suspect could be useful to you too. I've split them into categories.

1 - Design

I used to design and publish my own magazines and religiously used a combination of Indesign and MSPublisher. But now, whenever I need to create any socials, leaflets, documents or pretty much any asset that includes texts, video or images, I turn to Canva. I have the paid version because it gives me all the functionality I need but in the free version there's plenty there to keep most people busy.

2 - Email

Whilst more functionality has been included into Mailchimp I have to say the interface drives me nuts so I moved away to Flodesk instead which gives me the ability to create lead capture forms, beautiful and flexible emails, sequences and various other things - it works like a dream and is aesthetically very pleasing.

If I'm building websites that need CRM and email sequencing then I always turn to Sendly (all links are in the resources at the end). It gives me everything I need to create a beautiful looking site as well as the back end functionality to trigger email sequences, sales from an inbuilt store and so much more.

For my personal email I always make sure to have a proper domain (I use Fasthost to purchase these) and then feed them through a Gmail account so I can make use of Google tools such as the calendar etc.

3 - Communications

I have a business WhatsApp account which has proven really useful and I ensure that all my messages go through there so I only have one point of contact to check. I can run this both on my phone and also on my desktop.

4 - Security

For many years I have relied on Dashlane to store all of my passwords and I have it installed on all my devices. Not only is it entirely secure but it also saves me typing as it will autofill on any site that I go onto. I don't use anything else. And I thank the Lord for it every day as my menopausal brain doesn't want to remember stuff like this any more!

Chapter 10 Review and Actions - Some of my favourite systems

- Don't rule out good old fashioned pen and paper. These are really useful in many situations and helps your brain retain information.
- Digital systems are also a necessity for most businesses in some form or another so take your time to choose the right ones for your needs.

Chapter 11. It's about the non-negotiables

I am currently sat in the sun on a brief vacation in Greece and listening to a chap called Sean Conway being interviewed by Chris Evans on Radio 2. I have had the pleasure of meeting Sean a few years ago and have followed his journey, which today is day 102 of consecutive Iron-Man challenges. He is about to break a massive record and raise a lump of money for charity. It is Sean that has added some inspiration to this chapter together with a quote from Mike Tyson which is 'everyone has a plan until they get punched in the face'. Sean has had to employ various strategies to get him through this challenge. He described his ability to complete this as a series of 'non-negotiables' which he would not deviate from. For example, setting his alarm at 04:33 every morning irked him when he realised he was getting in the pool for the first stage at 05:01 so the alarm changed to 04:29 every morning and he would get straight out of bed, despite the temptation to hit the snooze button.

Getting into the ice bath, every day, was a non-negotiable. He wouldn't allow any door to be left partially open if it gave him the opportunity to miss one of these targets. And so, by doing these things every single day, without fail, he built up a set of habits which ensured his eventual success.

What can you do in your business that will enable you to reach your goals? It doesn't have to be setting your alarm for 04:29 but it could be that when your alarm goes off, instead of sitting in bed mindlessly scrolling, you get straight up and make yourself a healthy breakfast whilst reviewing your to-do list for the day.

It could be making sure that you go to bed at the same time every evening (this is really important) with a good book to give you proper time to wind down and relax before the next day.

It could be that you don't check any emails or messages until you have done the one needle moving activity required for the day. Whether it's writing some sales copy, raising your invoices, checking your cash flow etc, don't let the important thing slip into a pile of other things, because they get backed up in the list due to you doing the non-important stuff first.

Remember that this is your business and you can run it however you choose. When I set up my software firm I decided I didn't want it to look or feel anything like the corporate world I had come from. I needed to look professional and demonstrate that the software was robust, but the rest of it was down to me. So I had a policy of slippers in the office (after all, who wants to be stuck in outdoor shoes all day?).

We built a little kitchen where you could help yourself to tea and coffee, had sofas to relax on and a fish tank on the wall. The phones were answered by a trusted external company so that our developers and staff weren't disturbed unnecessarily (I hate an office with ringing phones ha ha!) and the vibe was very peaceful yet productive.

My non-negotiables looked like this:
- morning shower, without fail. I have my best ideas in a shower and it also gives me time to reset my head. Plus the energy from falling water does wonders for how you feel.
- cycle to work with my dog in the basket, to get fresh air and exercise.
- cups of tea. Obviously.
- Swim at lunchtime
- Plenty of water to drink
- Supplements and essential oils to support my emotional and physical health.

You'll soon start to create your own set of non-negotiable activities which will make a difference in your world if you genuinely stick to them and refuse to allow anything, or anyone, to derail you.

Now what about that quote I mentioned from Mike Tyson? I thought it was important because it doesn't matter how well planned your business is, or how much effort you've put into all eventualities, the fact is, at some point, you will be blindsided by something in life that will render you knocked out. This is just a fact - not many of us get through unscathed.

If you have your foundations set, with a series of non-negotiables, these will give you a huge advantage over everyone else. They will give you strength to keep going, to give you structure and provide reassurance that you'll get through.

Admittedly some of these 'face punches' will literally have you on the ground, flailing about, wondering what on earth happened. It's OK to take a bit of time to come back to your senses, be gentle on yourself and then have a good look around before you pull yourself up and get back on track. Without non-negotiables, you're likely to continue floundering, because there's no guide-rails to cling onto. People often ask me how I get so much done, or seem so organised. And the answer isn't particularly clever or that I've got special talents that others don't possess. The difference is that I have a set of non-negotiables that I swear by, which allow me to remain focussed on the goals and in fairness have become such ingrained habits that I almost struggle to list them such that they have become part of my DNA. It's a real effort for me to articulate how I do what I do, in the same way that you have to think about how you breathe. You can explain it but you have to have a bit of a think first!

Many of my clients are neuro-divergent. Generally these types of people really struggle to stick to routine or non-negotiables, and there's always an element of failure in their minds when they are unable to do this. And yet their brains fire off continuously with great ideas, creative thoughts and energy. With my work I allow them to stay in their zone of genius and I simply pull my non-negotiables into their world, giving them the backbone of strength and routine required in a business environment. So don't worry if you're one of these wonderful types and you feel like you procrastinate or your brain just struggles with certain activities, you can outsource help to ensure robustness in your world, even if it doesn't necessarily come directly from you. There's no shame in sticking up your hand and saying 'I need help' - if anything it's braver to do this than suffer in silence. Surround yourself with the biggest cheerleaders and advocates for what you do and you'll be far happier than slogging it out alone, comparing yourself to others who don't function in the same way and feeling like you'll never achieve. Remember that you have an equally valid set of skills - focus on these instead of beating yourself up about what you don't do brilliantly!

Write down here some of the non-negotiables that you feel should be part of your world:

Chapter 11 Review and Actions - It's all about the non-negotiables

- Take some time to really think about what your non-negotiable are in both your personal life and business. Which ones are most aligned with your core goals and values?
- Create a document or something that reminds you of these so that you don't deviate.

Chapter 12. So you want to be rich?

It is likely that you have started your business to make money. If not I would seriously question your motives because as I've said before, if your business isn't making money then you're simply running an expensive hobby. There is nothing wrong with being paid for your time and efforts, after all money is simply a physical exchange for these things and we all deserve to be paid for what we do.

So with that being said, have you had a thought about how much money you want to earn? I hear so many business owners excitedly forecasting their turnover, knowing the total target market globally and saying 'if I could just get 1% of that then I'll be a squillionaire. I just have to scale' etc, blah.

If you actually got 'only 1%' then you will be doing amazingly well. The reality is that you're not likely to get this, in fact it's likely to be far less. So get a big fat rubber out and change your forecast. I'm not going to be a Debbie Downer on you, but get started with something more realistic whilst you find your feet. Setting goals that are most likely unachievable will only make you feel shit in the face of what could be rather palpable success. Only you won't see it that way because it won't have hit the mark on your spreadsheet.

I can't tell you how many business owners I've inwardly yawned at when they've told me they're running a 6-figure company and then I've asked what their profit is, and then what they're paying themselves. Turnover is a great KPI but is absolutely not necessarily a measure of success nor is it indicative of stability.

>Profit is.
>The way you manage the business is.
>Your financial reality is.

If you buy into the whole coaching bollocks of 'sit in the car you're going to buy' then please, for the love of the God of sanity, remember this is part of a manifestation and visualisation exercise, not some ticket into a club you can't yet afford. Many business owners, swept up in the excitement of their future success, think that by taking out a huge overhead for a car they can't afford, it will give them some sort of kudos. No. This is the equivalent of going into your mums closet, putting on her shoes and pretending to be grown up. The only outcome of this is that at some point you'll be told to put them back until you're ready and you'll end up feeling a bit silly and stop doing it, and have a load of blisters to boot.

I genuinely want you to be successful. I genuinely want you to carve out a business that makes sense to you and your family, whether that's a whole heap of fur babies, rug rats or your closest friends. I do not want this to come at the cost of your sanity or health because you're chasing a figure from the outset that you're simply not ready to chase.

Think of it a bit like an airplane taking off. It needs a huge amount of fuel and thrust to get into the air.

All its energy is focussed on taking flight. Nothing else is happening at this point apart from safely getting into the air (as an aside, the first 40 seconds of flight are apparently the most dangerous. As a frightened flier that was an important point to note. Anyway, I digress...). The plane doesn't just shoot up like a rocket though. It goes up in stages, a bit like a flight of stairs. It does one stage at a time all the while focussed on its ultimate target of 35,000 feet. If it tried to get to 35,000 feet in one go it would fail because it has to go through these stages to get there.

Your business is no different. Set the big goal, by all means, but take it in steps. Give it all you've got to get there, because once you've hit altitude then you can take the thrust off and start cruising. Your engines still need to run and the team onboard still need to keep things running smoothly. You may have to divert due to bad weather or medical issues but if you've got your non-negotiables in place (engine maintenance, staff training and whatever other things they do on aircraft!) you'll weather the storm and be ready to go again.

Let's take some time to have another think about how much money needs to come in and out of your business in order that you can a) get paid, b) cover the outgoings and c) grow. Think back to the chapter where we explored your numbers. I'm sure there were some gems in that one and you're in a better position to be thinking about how you can improve this area. But step aside from the reality of your current situation and let's take a look at what you NEED to be achieving.

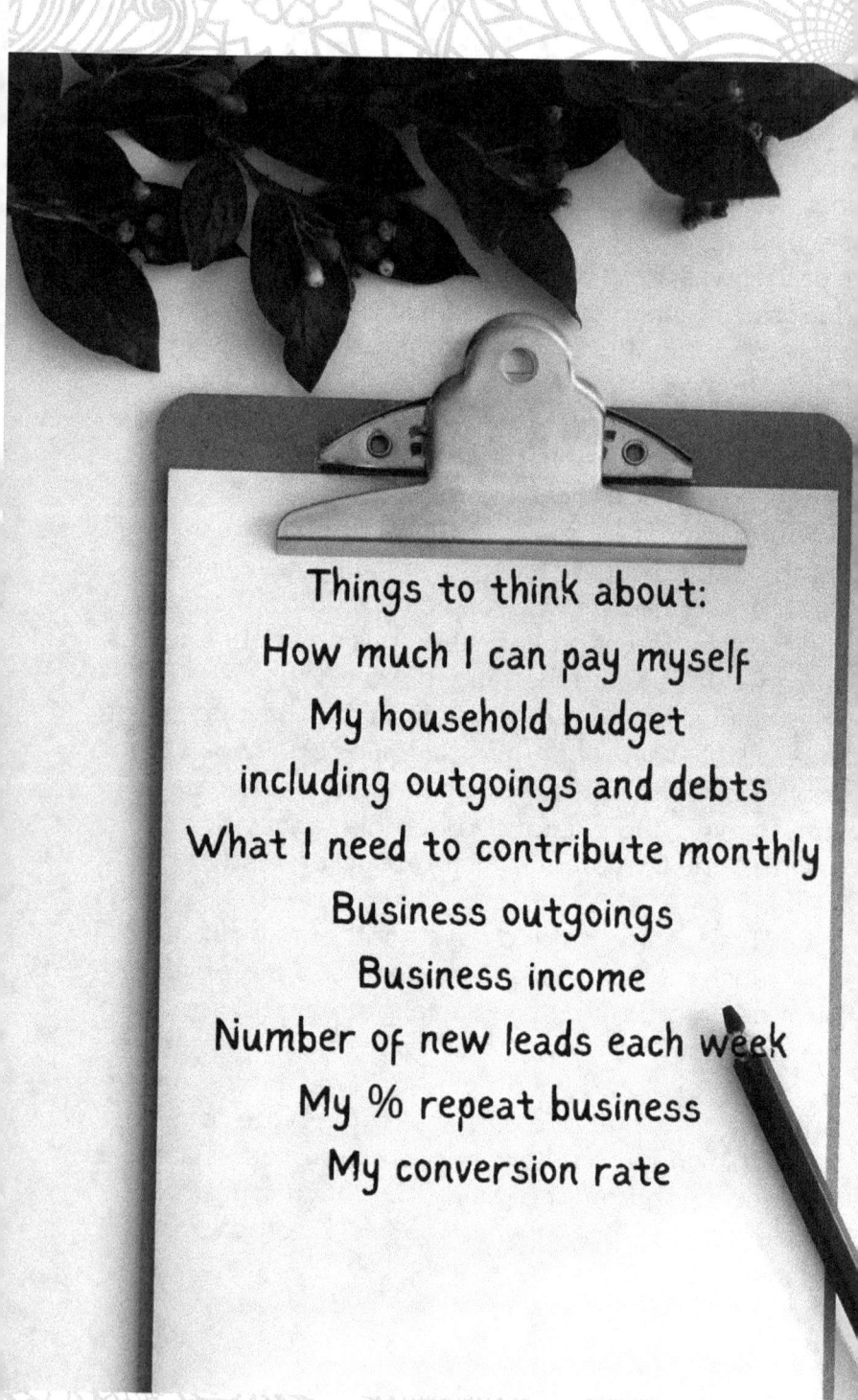

So, back to the title of this chapter. I firmly believe in being paid for what you do but I also firmly believe in giving. Giving to others, caring about them and having a genuine desire to make things better is way more important than money itself. The two things should go hand in hand in business and there is no embarrassment to say you earn money doing something you love, that helps people. BUT.... Do you want to be rich? Or do you want to be wealthy?

In my mind there's a subtle difference.

To me, being rich generally involves high overheads and keeping up with the Joneses. There may be a job that you have to keep doing to support your lifestyle and you may be constantly worried about performance or work stability. But by being wealthy, you don't have these worries. Being wealthy gives you financial independence. You choose to work when you want to and if you don't want to, or can't, it doesn't matter. You are not necessarily supporting a lavish lifestyle but the lifestyle you choose can function whether you are working or not.

Consider whether the lifestyle you are aspiring to falls into the rich, or wealthy category.

I personally choose wealthy.

'Many people think that being rich and being wealthy are the same thing. But there is a difference between the two. The rich have lots of money but the wealthy don't worry about money'.

Chapter 12 Review and Actions - So you want to be rich?

- Spend some time thinking about your budget and your business KPI's that are realistic and focussed on your core goals.
- Do you want to be rich? Or do you want to be wealthy?

Chapter 13. 86400

One thing which I've learned is that by going flat out and nearly killing yourself, you don't guarantee a place at the table of riches just because you've pulled many all-nighters and missed most of your kids school performances. There are no medals to be won in the game of life here for martyrdom. All that happens is you miss time you'll never be able to get back and then you have to juggle the balls of guilt and exhaustion whilst pushing yourself onwards to meet your goals. This, people, is not sustainable and not life. OK, reality check - there will be moments in business (and life in general) when you have to make sacrifices and pull out all the stops in order to make that 'thing' happen but these should be exceptions rather than the rule. I am speaking here from years of not taking my own medicine and as a result my body eventually made the decision for me, rendering me exhausted and ill for over 6 months where I did very little other than go to the loo or make a cup of tea. I slept the other 23 hours. I continue to deal with the after-effects of years of mental and physical neglect and will happily preach to anybody that will listen that it IS NOT WORTH IT!!!!!

I am genuinely not exaggerating when I tell you that as a result of parenting 5 beautiful children, moving and renovating more houses than I can list, running multiple businesses and various other major life events, I broke. And the only reason this happened was because I thought I could just keep going. I thought that I could do what I did in my younger years and my body would sustain me even though I did very little to support it. I burned out, became ill, developed ME and various other autoimmune issues that you cannot just 'cure'. Thankfully my work with natural health has allowed me to reverse most of these and put them into 'management' but trust me, I wish I didn't have to do that. I wish that I could exercise for more than 3 days in a row without ending up in bed. I wish I didn't have the most irritating, soul-destroying psoriasis on my scalp that I work incredibly hard to keep at bay. I wish I didn't have the beginnings of arthritis in my hands from constantly being at my keyboard. I wish I didn't have very obvious signs of ageing now from the immense amount of stress I have put myself through. The list goes on and all of these will continue to impact my world without my rigorous intervention through lifestyle changes. I can't just breeze through like before.

    The bottom line is, I didn't get the balance right. I am an epic manager of time and I challenge anyone to do more work and juggle more things than I do/have done. Yet now I know that's not the best way to be. As I discussed in Chapter 7, prioritising the things that may not be needle moving activities is incredibly important because it will allow you to do the needle moving activities for longer! Setting up your non-negotiables to include downtime, wellness, good food and sleep will make you more of a machine during the periods you need to work. Trying to be a machine for 18 hours of every day will ultimately kill you. And most likely you'll be miserable because everyone around you who loves you won't see you.

   Just for clarity, I am not saying don't work hard. I'm not saying that you shouldn't excitedly pour everything you have into your work. And that there are times when you really have to give that all of your focus because of the Mike Tyson face-punches that will come your way. But if you've managed yourself and your time well, you'll be stronger and better equipped to deal with those knock-out punches. So staying at the office late, working weekends and refusing to take a break at lunch is not the way to do it on an everyday basis. We are not in the hustle-culture of the '90's any more. You do not need to be attached to your phone 24/7 and if you are I strongly suggest getting a second work phone that you leave in your drawer 'after hours'. Time is the one commodity that we cannot get back. Once it is spent, we can't 'un-spend' it. It is the most precious thing, with the exception of your health, that you will ever have because you don't know how much you have got.

   Here's the shocker. We all have the same amount of time. 86400 seconds in a day given to those of us lucky enough to wake up again in the morning. How we choose to use that time can dictate our future successes. And on an 80 year life that's only 4000 weeks and 960 months if we are blessed.

   Time management can be a real challenge for so many of us because 'tomorrow' is always an option, until it's not. And for those of us who see and manage time in a different way it's often difficult to guide you with my methodologies because they simply won't work. Being surrounded by neurodiverse people in my family and clientele, I thought it appropriate to include my tips here for you to help you stay organised and productive:

- stop writing everything in random places (scraps of paper, different notebooks, digital notes) and then wondering why you can't find anything. Have ONE diary with dates printed and write things into the day. DO NOT DEVIATE! Consider getting a Remarkable or Kindle Scribe so that you have one device, that still allows you to write things down, but that copies everything into the digital atmosphere allowing you to have everything where you need it, when you need it.
- Outsource anything that you cannot focus on and do this with a sense of empowerment and delegation, rather than failure. You need to work in your zone of genius and staying in the guard rails is unlikely to be one of those zones!
- If you've carried on reading to this third point I'm proud… keep going…

For everyone else here are some more tips that I have employed on a daily basis (and trust me, I've had to sit and think really hard about these because, as I mentioned earlier in this book, these are things I do now without really thinking about them!)

- Keep a paper diary on your desk. And use it. Committing things to paper commits things into your brain but in a different way to digital. Imagine the information flow like a two way feed. Digital tends to be one way. Writing things down helps you download things from your brain but you also, bizarrely, remember them better when you've used a pen. Use this as an opportunity to buy gorgeous stationery and fabulous pens and actually use them to whatever extent serves you. (For me, I love nothing more than a Hobinichi Cousin, A5 for my work diary. The paper is the most delicious, crinkly, soft-printed grid style and I get a great deal of joy from using it). It serves a dual purpose - I log my meetings in there and also the 'to-do' list for the day.
- Add important meetings from your paper diary to a digital option (google or iCal) and set alarms if needed so you don't miss these. If you want something aesthetically pleasing then I have used Artful Agenda which gives you push reminders, digital stickers and allows you to sync it with your google calendar (for example) so you don't have to look at the boring app and instead curate something far nicer on your pc or phone).
- Use the 'next three things' strategy. This is something I've employed fairly recently and I have to say it's genius. Previously I had a 'to do' list which I would create for the following day. I'd cross through all the completed tasks and then roll any unfinished to the following day or next appropriate slot. Then the following morning I would review what I had to do, add anything else to it that was required, work

through it, review at the end of the day and then rinse and repeat. The 'next three things' strategy is slightly different and might help you to see a to-do list in a totally unique way.

Here's an image of one of mine:

You can see that it is a combination of a mind-map style and a list.

What I do each morning is create a box in the middle that says 'today/date' and from here I draw a line to another heading that could be, for example, the name of a client or a topic. Underneath that heading will be a list of all the things I need to achieve for that client in that day. Alternatively it could be 'launch retreat' as the goal and then underneath that would be all the things I need to do that day for that goal. Map out everything that you need to do in that format, not worrying about any order that you write it down, or whereabouts it appears on the page. It can just be a random flow of actions that are grouped together for each goal.

Make sure to leave space on the page for the next bit.

Create a heading called 'first three'.

Underneath this, pull out the first three things you need to do that day, no matter which goal they link to. Against each of these, add one, two or three dots to denote speed of task. One dot is a quick job, two dots longer and three dots is more detailed. You get the idea.

Only once these three tasks are completed and ticked off do you get to write in the next heading, which is 'next three'. Pull out the next three things which need doing, allocate the timing dots again and do those.

Keep going until you either run out of time, or tasks. Those that don't get done need to be pushed out to another day.

You might wonder why this is a good process. Having used it I've learned that this is really helpful for several reasons:

- 1 - It stops overwhelm. Instead of looking at an endlessly long list, you've only got three tasks to worry about.

- 2 - It helps you be realistic about how much work you can get done - assessing the length of a task is a skill and one which will only improve with experience - but most people think they can do more in a day than they actually do.

- 3 - It stops procrastination. You set your goal of three tasks and therefore you're not staring at a long list trying to decide which one to do next. You've already made that decision first thing in the morning. If your procrastination levels are high and you can't even get to the point of creating your 'first three' then there's always a reason. It's either there's something you don't want to do so you don't want to write it down, or you're disinterested or more worryingly you're suffering with anxiety/depression. Procrastination is an emotional problem and not a time management problem, although this is the area in which it is observed. Managing negative mood around a task can be helped with recognising that you're procrastinating and instead of beating yourself up about it, give yourself a bit of love and say 'ok, I hear you! We've got this!'. Have a look at the task that is causing you this feeling and instead of ploughing straight in (which you're not going to do because you're procrastinating), ask yourself what little bit you could do to get started, if you chose to. Research from Dr Phchyl says that focusing on the next action will help calm your nerves and allows for a layer of 'self-deception'. You can consider the next action to be a possibility, as if you were method acting. By taking the first baby step, motivation will follow, as it always does by taking action.

◉ If you're visual it helps you to see a list in both ways - as a list and as a diagram so your left and right brain will both be happy!

◉ It gives you a chance to time block by only estimating for three things at a time. There's a tendency when doing a whole list that your brain will fudge the estimates because of the need to complete that list in one day. That's a bit like trying to fit your size 14 arse into a pair of size 8 jeans. Sadly it's not going to happen and the bits you do manage to squeeze in will find a way of bulging out and looking very unattractive. Not how you want your lovely to-do list to be!

There are some other tips here that I'd like to suggest that you also consider.

- If you only had 10 hours a week to run your business I guarantee you'd do away with some of the tasks that you think are 'crucial' now, but really aren't.

- Learn to say 'no'. This one has taken me a very long time to learn and women in particular are bad at doing this for fear of people thinking they can't cope / they don't like them etc. Being able to lovingly say no to things, and yes to the stuff that is in alignment with your goals and aspirations, and anything that makes your heart and soul sing is empowering and important.

- Take time for rest and exercise. It will make your focus at work stronger and you'll have better ideas. Without fail I shower every single morning and all of my best thoughts have come from being in the shower. From new companies to life thoughts, my cubicle has become a ritual that is an absolute non-negotiable because I know it sets my day up with the best possible chance for success.

- Your cognitive function decreases with lack of sleep. You'll experience poor attention span, reduced adaptability, reduced emotional capacity, impaired judgement and will go on to make poor diet choices, oftentimes turning to sugar, to keep you from feeling tired. Then you'll have a sugar 'high' followed by a crash, you'll feel more exhausted so reach for the sugar or the caffeine and then onto the rollercoaster bus you go. Toodle pips.

* Make sure you prioritise sleep above all else. You can download a sleep protocol that I use during sleep classes (yep - I teach people how to sleep it's that important!) by visiting my instagram @themamabearceo.

* Don't expect to fit in the same amount of work as your friend if you have 2 kids and she has none. Don't beat yourself up if your friend seems to be running faster than you if she's got staff including a cleaning lady and admin assistant. We all have different journeys and what things can look like from the outside can be very different to what is going on from the inside. With one of my companies I decided quite quickly in that we were like the Wizard of Oz. We (somehow unintentionally) gave the illusion that we were much bigger than we were. There was an expectation that we had big shiny offices and lots of staff. The professional portrayal of the outward-facing marketing led people to believe something that they had decided to be true. None of the marketing was fabricated but assumptions were quickly made. We can all do that about others - try not to because oftentimes you'll be way off the mark. I always remember a really funny scenario which I'll share with you now which involved a series of phone calls. My partner, Sean, used to deal with the accounts in all our companies. He took a call from a customer in the States to discuss an issue and thought it was resolved. The same chap phoned back the following day with some other issue and Sean answered the phone. He gave him the answer that was needed but the chap was insistent that it

wasn't the answer he was looking for and could he talk to the gentleman from the day before, because he was much more helpful? Amusingly (Sean was in a mischievous mood that day), he put the call on hold, walked into another room and answered saying 'hello, this is Sean, how can I help?'. They had another conversation and the chap left the call feeling delighted that his needs had been met!

I'm not advocating of course that you pretend to be different people EXCEPT in one scenario. And that's credit control. If you're a one man band it becomes very difficult to have an exchange of energies with someone who then decides they can't or won't pay. Chasing the money down, for a lot of people, feels awkward and this is where having a 'good cop, bad cop' routine is perfect. Create yourself another email address for accounts and have the signature with a different name. 'Polly' can now happily go about chasing your debt whilst you hide behind your pseudonym feeling a little bit more protected from this type of work.

* set up systems to save you time. My favourites are:
- meal planning
- Home organisation hacks (hallway command centre, clutter free living and everything labelled)
- Home management folder which contains all the key information needed to run your home and key dates such as insurances for home and vehicles, mot dates etc. It's really easy to grab this folder and sync any reminders for these things into your diaries

rather than go rummaging about wasting time trying to find this information.
- Weekly food deliveries so you don't waste time in supermarkets, spend more than you need and only purchase what's required from your meal plan. Or try and go shopping locally with a list of what you need and support your local businesses.

My last thoughts on this (very large) topic are this. Time is a slippery bugger and we all think we have more of it than we actually do. Whether we're in our 20's feeling young and indestructible or in our 50's wondering how the heck we got here and still feeling 20-something, the next day isn't guaranteed. Every day should contain something that makes you happy, even if there are tasks you have to do that are a bit 'meh' (like taking out the bins). Life is way too short to be doing something because you think you should, or because other people think you should.
  Imagine if you were on your death bed now and you were asked how you would have lived your life differently if you could.

Now take that answer and go do it.

Chapter 13 Review and Actions - 86400

- Breaking yourself is not cool. We are no longer in the 1980's or 90's where hustle-culture and 'I can work more hours than you' should be celebrated.
- Setting up your non-negotiable is important to make sure you include wellness, downtime, good food and sleep - make sure that your list includes these things for success.
- Consider the organisational and productive tips suggested and how you may be able to implement these into your world.
- Set up the time saving systems you need to help you in both your home and business life.

Chapter 14. Numbers & Feelings

If I see the number 13 appear then my superstitious senses start tingling and I know that all is right in the world! It's a number which pops up quite a lot for me (one could argue it's because it's on my radar but I like to think it's special!). So as we are on the subject of magic numbers I thought we could conclude this book with my thoughts about how life can be wrapped up.

And really it comes down to one of two things. It's either by numbers, or by feelings.

Imagine that you are ready to pass on to your next journey. You are laying in your bed, hopefully free of pain and you are thinking back over the life you have been blessed with.

What will you be thinking?

I bet it comes down to feelings. Experiences you have enjoyed (or not) and how they made you feel. Things you have done that have made others feel a certain way. The tingle in the back of your neck when you first start a new relationship, or the warmth on your skin when you step off an aircraft in the summer sun.

Then you'll think of the numbers. Did you have enough
- Love
- Holidays
- Life
- Fun
- Friendships
- Passion

- Success
- Meaning

Did you give enough
- Love
- Friendship
- Care
- Passion
- Compassion

But perhaps instead of waiting until those last, precious moments, you think about the balance of your world.

Where are you lacking in the list above? Circle those that apply.

What would you choose to do if you had a free day that was free of responsibility or worry?

Write it down on the next page. Dream away and imagine all the things that YOU would choose to do if you weren't thinking of your partner/work/kids etc. Dream bigger and think about what you'd do if money were no object. What would you eat? What would you wear? How would you feel? Who would you be with?

Now let me ask you a question.
Why are you waiting?
What is stopping you?

You are creating a life by design by owning your own business. If you can't carve out time to do the things you love then the balance is wrong somewhere. Don't get sucked into the trap of feeling like you have to spend more money than you can afford on houses, cars and 'stuff' that will keep you in debt and further away from the freedom you are craving. Work out how you can live on less, with less, so that ultimately you have more.

Remember what we learned in this book.

There have been lots of lessons but here is a little recap:

Where you are now

Look at your personality and play to your strengths. Don't waste time fannying about with stuff that you'll probably always hate and find hard.

Think about your ultimate goal and consider whether you're in limbo land and what you're risking by staying here.

Sorting out your fears

Take some time to look at what is actually scaring you and whether this is really a problem at all.

Is your ultimate goal rooted in success or have you not considered some of the SMART steps to take when you created it?

Pick just one self care priority and focus on that until it's sorted.

Sorting out your environment

Look at where you're working. Are you perched on the end of the kitchen table? If you employed you, would you continue to do so by working like this?!

Make some changes to how and where you work for maximum success and satisfaction.

Think about removing negative media/people from your world and spending time with people or things that bring joy.

Get control of your numbers

Stop abdicating control of your figures to someone else and use my simple exercise to get on top of your key business numbers, plus save money at the same time.

Get hold of my step by step course to simplify this by visiting me @themamabearceo on Instagram.

Deal with the stress

Sometimes it can all feel like too much. Let's take stock of where you are and get the stressors sorted out, once and for all by picking the lowest hanging fruit.

Are you stuck in perturbation?

Is your life like a pan on the boil, neither boiling hard or cooling down? Are you in a limbo state with your business and don't know which way to turn? Think about the non-negotiable that will set you apart from other businesses and make a decision to move, one way or the other.

Sort your systems!

We looked at systems and processes and what these actually mean in terms of your business. Spend time defining what it is you're trying to achieve and then match the software or manual system to this.

Remember to sense check regularly any system you put in place otherwise rubbish in = rubbish out!

Don't rule out pen and paper either. Despite the acceleration of digital technology these still have a place.

Set your non-negotiables
And jolly well stick to them!

Do you want to be rich?
Why are you doing all this, after all? Are you looking for a job, or something that can create wealth?

The most valuable asset - time
We all have the same amount of it and yet we all seem to approach time with a different attitude. So many of us break ourselves because we don't prioritise the right things, and then wish that we could rewind time and do things differently. Some of us are too scared to use time well because of worry about what 'might happen'. None of us really knows how much time we actually have but the chances are, if you woke up this morning you've got a delicious 86400 seconds to do something NOW for you and your life. Don't waste any of them worrying, or by spending it with things or people that aren't important. Prioritise the right things and only bring things into your world that you choose.

Life is for the taking.
You are worth so much and every day should be special.
It won't be easy.
But you can do it if you want it badly enough.
Step into your new world and go live.

And remember above all else…. You too can be the Mama Bear of your own world. Love with honesty, protect your world fiercely and move through life with grace and joy.

Much love

Coralie

Some lessons in images

Opening my first conference as MD of my software business. Public speaking is NOT my forte but I prepared, put my big girl pants on and did it anyway. The more I did, the easier it got. (Easier, not necessarily better!).

Love your customers. If there isn't a place for them to be recognised, do it yourself. We set up an annual awards for all of ours so that they had a level playing field to be acknowledged.

Chatting with the late Richard Denny (above) who was keynote at one of our annual conferences and on stage presenting awards with Sean (and Oscar) at an evening event that we set up to recognise Independent Publishers.

With the late Ruby and Boo, both my precious rescue Bichons. Ruby was a precious princess and Boo looked like she had been abusing drugs most of her life but we adored them both.

With Sean, my rock, on one of our many travel adventures, this time to the USA. I might hate flying but I won't let it stop me!

On Ronnie Rebel my trusty steed who has seen many adventures from camping trips to sunrises and sunsets. Nothing beats the feeling of freedom and I'll always think of my precious late brother, Mark, who was an exceptional rider and volunteered his time to be a Blood Rider delivering urgent supplies of blood throughout Wales.

Acknowledgements

Being able to write a book like this doesn't come down to just sitting at a desk and churning out a few words. It has come as a result of a lifetime of work, experiences and relationships and so I wanted to acknowledge some of mine here because they have contributed to getting me where I am today.

First of all, my partner Sean who has been by my side for 16 years and should have been there from the start. You jumped in with both feet, eyes wide open and have been my biggest cheerleader, always ready with a smile and a hug and the right words to sort out my ever-doubting mind. I love you.

Then my sister, Sally, who without a doubt has been one of my biggest reasons for doing so much, from jacking in a job that was killing me, to getting on with some of my crazy ideas when I thought I wasn't good enough. You are tenacious and I'm so very proud of all the amazing things you have done in your world.

To my first-born, Lauren, who made me a mum and taught me how to juggle even more than I thought was possible, and whose very presence and demanding smile got me through some very dark times. You know you're my favourite first daughter. And of course I have to mention Toby, Max, Lucy and Ava, my precious kids who drive me to distraction but never cease to surprise me every day with the way you're growing up. Toby, I know you'll find your true path one day. Keep smiling and the light will shine for you. Max, it goes without saying that you are just like your Dad. But you're also you. Don't lose that magic smile and listen to your heart. Being true to yourself will take you where you want to be. Lucy, your soul shines when you smile. Keep the lightheartedness of your true self and the world will be kind to you. You have a crazy and blessed life ahead of you. And Ava, you'll always be my special cat. Just make sure you find the right lap to sit in and the world will be your oyster.

Then I want to acknowledge some business greats who contributed to my journey. First of all my coach, Ian Dickson, who has always, without fail, offered his support, extensive tool kit and guidance whenever I have reached out. You are a gentleman and a fabulous coach. Never forget that.

To the late Richard Denny, who Sean and I had the pleasure of sharing some time with at our conferences and later his home, before he sadly passed on. I have never met such a generous, funny, clever and polite chap who was very clear about telling me that "you can always make more money, Coralie, but you can never make more time". Thank you for the advise you gave us. It meant more than you will ever know.

And then to Sháá Wasmund who got me started on a journey of self care when I attended The One Retreat many years ago. You gave me permission to look at myself as important, fed me amazing vegan food and juices and let me properly snot-blub all over you when you managed to verbally poke me in just the right way to let it all out. I am so glad that you
  have found someone special again and you are rocking being a working mum. Thank you.

To all my customers, past and present. It has been an honour to work with, and for you. I hope you know that everything I do is to try and make your worlds better and I will continue to do that, as best as I can. I will continue to nag and nurture you so that you don't have a 'car crash' moment because it's easier for me to see it coming that you. I'll always be your Mama-Bear and defend you from yourself and others!

    Lastly to my soul-dog, Ruby, who literally stayed by my side every day of her life, gazing up at me to see what was happening next, who happily rode every day in the basket of my bike. I hope you're up on a cloud looking down and that you know how much your little chops meant to me.

Resources

Paper planners
- The Daily Grind - www.thedailygrindplanner.com
- Hobonichi - ranges are available from Amazon, The Journal Shop, Nishura East.

Digital planners
Remarkable - https://remarkable.com
Artful Agenda - https://artfulagenda.com/

CRM and email systems
- For web building, sales and more - www.sendly.co.uk (soon to be rebranded as hublo)
- For beautiful emails, lead generation tools and sequences - www.flodesk.com
- For more complex CRMs look at www.infusionsoft.com

Organisation and team collaboration tools
- For organising nearly everything - www.trello.com
- A combination of Pinterest meets Trello - www.milanote.com
- Teamwork is a great tool for managing teams

Design tools
www.canva.com

Security tools
www.dashlane.com

Social media and video
- For recording your screen and sharing video - www.loom.com
- For mapping out your social content and great for tips and ideas try www.plann.com
- For great video editing try Final Cut Pro or Camtasia

Online Stores
- www.sendly.co.uk
- www.shopify.com

Lead Generation
Create beautiful quizzes and surveys with www.typeform.com
Use Flodesk or Sendly for lead capture boxes and email sequences

Accounts packages
All super easy for small business owners to use and manage:
www.freeagent.com
www.xero.com